ON THE HUNT FOR THE HAUNTED

About the Author

Robin M. Strom has been researching and investigating the paranormal for the better part of a decade. During that time, she has written extensively on the subject of ghosts for her blog, *The Shore*, at delawareparanormal.blogspot.com. She is the founder and director of Delaware Paranormal Research Group. She is a teacher of English, communications, and broadcasting and was a television journalist. Aside from video, she is also an enthusiastic amateur photographer. She loves anything to do with the water, jogging, hiking, biking, drinking Bloody Marys (piña coladas being far too sweet), and getting caught in the rain. She lives in Delaware with her husband, son, Uther Pendogin the dog, Miss Scarlet the cat, and a sugar glider named Hiccup.

Searching for Proof of the Paranormal

ON THE HUNT FOR THE HAUNTED

ROBIN M. STROM

Llewellyn Publications
Woodbury, Minnesota

FIRST EDITION
First Printing, 2019

Book design by Samantha Penn
Cover design by Kevin R. Brown
Cover illustration by Dominick Finelle / The July Group
Interior photos provided by the author

Library of Congress Cataloging-in-Publication Data (Pending)
ISBN: 978-0-7387-5841-1

Llewellyn Publications
A Division of Llewellyn Worldwide Ltd.
2143 Wooddale Drive
Woodbury, MN 55125.2989
www.llewellyn.com

Printed in the United States of America

Also by Robin M. Strom

Anatomy of a Ghost:
A Guide to Analyzing the Dead

This book is dedicated to my dad, whom I miss every day. I did it, Dad! Oh, and the Cubs won the World Series. Really, I'm not kidding.

CONTENTS

Acknowledgments

Special thanks to Renne Whitmore and Judy Hill-Truitt for helping me with the research for this book. If I needed a sexual offender profiled or the history of an old hotel researched, they were kind enough to do it. Thank you both for your invaluable assistance. I could not have done it without you.

INTRODUCTION

To understand the living, you got to commune with the dead.
—Minerva, *Midnight in the Garden of Good and Evil*

I am a paranormal researcher and have been for a number of years. That means while most *normal* people are off for a walk or mowing the lawn, I'm in my house behind a computer screen perusing long hours of video, listening to audio, researching, or writing. I miss a lot of family time. My rosebushes are woefully overgrown, and we end up eating more meals of takeout than I like to admit. It's not glamorous. I wish I could say, as an author, that I got into the paranormal because I'd been terrorized by an evil demon as a child or had grown up in a haunted house, fighting for my very existence. But my formative years were peaceful and joyous. I had my own first paranormal experience when I was in my early thirties, and that wasn't terrifying either—just mystifying, as so many paranormal phenomena tend to be.

However, I've always had a taste for the macabre, enjoying ghost stories as a child and scary movies as a teen. For me, that's all they had ever been—just stories. I don't know that I ever fathomed that the paranormal could actually be real until that first time I experienced it. And I certainly never considered that I might be able to study the paranormal until that one fateful night I saw my first *Ghost Hunters* episode.

Certainly, I got into paranormal research seeking to experience something. But the reason I think it bit me so hard and fast was the fact that at the very bottom of all this work and time was the pursuit of fundamental answers. Is there life beyond death? Are ghosts real? If so, what are they? The quest for those answers has kept me going all these years.

I can say that I now know that odd, frightening, and unexplainable things happen to people, perfectly normal people, every day. People of all ages, socioeconomic levels, education levels, and religious backgrounds. Experiences with the paranormal are universal across cultures and societies. And people have paranormal experiences more often than you'd expect. Recent polls suggest that three-quarters of the American population believe in the possibility of the paranormal, and nearly one in five claim to have seen a ghost.[1] Still greater is the number of people who report that they have felt that they had been in touch with a loved one who had recently died (29 percent). These encounters don't necessarily involve witnessing an apparition, but they can include hearing the voice of a deceased person, feeling a touch, smelling a distinctive odor associated with the deceased, sensing a presence, or witnessing what they interpret as a sign. Further, over one-third of the population

---

1. David Robson, "Psychology: The Truth about the Paranormal," BBC Future, October 31, 2014, http://www.bbc.com/future/story/20141030-the-truth-about-the-paranormal.

believes in life after death, and nearly as many believe that a building can be haunted.[2]

Our Approach

As I said earlier, I got into paranormal research because I was searching for answers. As a result, I try to remain unbiased when I approach an investigation. I don't want to delude myself that a place is haunted if it's not, and I certainly don't wish to mislead my clients. They contact me for help, and I can only help them if I give them the most accurate information I can. Delaware Paranormal Research Group therefore uses a more scientific approach to paranormal investigation than the vast majority of my paranormal colleagues. To be brief but clear, we don't use psychics to give readings of a location, we don't hold séances, and we don't use Ouija boards or ghost boxes. Instead, we use an arsenal of electronic equipment in order to record and detect anything that's going on at a location.

I have had clients who really didn't want us to employ a scientific approach to an investigation. Many of them really just want me to bring in a medium to give them a reading. And I understand where they are coming from. But I can't verify a feeling or an impression—it isn't solid material proof—and I begin my *own* journey looking for that proof.

To obtain that proof we basically use three broad categories of equipment: measurement devices, recording devices, and detection devices. Our measurement devices measure environmental changes, monitoring temperature, barometric pressure, electromagnetic fields, vibration, humidity, and so on. Of course, the most prosaic device is

2. Michael Lipka, "18% of Americans Say They've Seen a Ghost," Pew Research Center, October 30, 2015, http://www.pewresearch.org/fact-tank/2015/10/30/18-of-americans-say-theyve-seen-a-ghost/.

the electromagnetic field (EMF) detector. Electromagnetic fields are everywhere around us all the time. The human brain is powered by electromagnetism, and so are the muscles that move our arms and legs. There's a natural EMF in both the core of the earth and your household lamp. Ghosts are believed to be willful energy, a consciousness without a body. In order to have an interaction with us or to fuel activity, they need to feed themselves with energy just as we eat food. It's long been supposed that they can do this by draining energy from household electrical devices (AC power) or from battery-powered devices (DC power). When they do something like bang on a wall or speak into a recorder, they are expending that energy. Hence, the EMF detector is an essential in every tool kit, just as a carpenter always has a hammer.

With such a useful tool, why do we bother with mundane environmental measurements like temperature? Well, while a change in the EMF is often associated with paranormal activity, it isn't *always*, and there are other environmental sources of energy that a spirit might tap into as well.

Recording devices are just what they sound like. The team has an essential surveillance camera system that records in daylight and in infrared at night. Infrared is the part of the light spectrum just below our field of vision. We also have smaller, independent video cameras for stationary use or carrying with us. Audio recorders are also placed in rooms in the hopes of catching an electronic voice phenomenon (EVP), which is a voice captured on the recording but not heard during the investigation.

Our detection devices sound an alarm or indicate an immediate change in a location. We employ motion sensors, and REM Pods and Mel Meters alert us if something has broken the field.

Evidence Review

First and foremost, the team is tasked with finding reasonable explanations for events. Is an EMF spike caused by a man-made device or a ghost? A cold spot is likely to be a leaky window or open flue on a fireplace. If we hear the creaking of a floorboard, we will try to recreate it. We also take into account the time of year and weather patterns. High humidity makes wood floors swell and doors stick. Changes in temperature can make them pop.

When it comes to evidence that I present to a client, it's all about what we have captured and can verify. If we capture a clearly audible EVP, a voice that we cannot account for, that is evidence I can present to a client. If one of our detection devices sounds an alarm announcing a change in the environment at the same time we capture an EVP, that's a stronger indication that something paranormal is going on. It's even better if one of the team members reports a personal experience, such as feeling chills on one arm, at the same time the EMF detector indicates a change in EMF, and we capture an EVP moments later. I especially like situations where we can layer the evidence to build a stronger argument for something paranormal occurring. Certainly, there are times when we experience nothing in an investigation and capture nothing on our recording devices.

Once we have conducted an investigation, we begin our evidence-review phase, in which we check data logger data, watch all the video feeds, listen to all the audio we recorded, and carefully analyze anything we caught that was anomalous. It is a mind-numbing process that takes several people many hours to accomplish, as every bit of audio and video has to be reviewed in real time and then compared to other video or audio for verification. We conduct research into the property as well, to try to find its history. That often involves calls to town hall offices and trips to the local historical society. From start to finish, one investigation usually takes the team and me one month to a month and a half from initial contact to final reveal. It's truly a labor of love.

In the accounts of the five investigations included in the book, I've added the inhabitants' description of the paranormal activity, any history of the property that might be relevant, a description of our investigation, and the evidence we found thereafter. As a haunted building remains a haunted building even after we've conducted our investigation, I've added updates (if I have them) that describe anything recent that's occurred at the property.

Much of what I amass in my research is anecdotal—in other words, stories from people who felt they'd had a paranormal experience. Obviously, stories shared long after they occurred are flawed as evidence: first, because our memory of events is extremely poor, and second, because events that are not recorded can't really be considered evidence. Still, accounts of paranormal activity can be useful when looking for similarities in activity. Also, some of the most haunted locations are the most private or inaccessible. There's no way I'll be given clearance to a working hospital, for example, in order to access the World War I–era nurse who has been witnessed in the basement. Some people don't wish me to intrude on their lives with a trunk-load of electronic equipment and a team of strangers. Often an event was a one-time occurrence, so setting up a full investigation would be a waste of time. But people are often willing to share their stories, and from these stories I can sometimes find correlations with other investigations I have conducted. So, while I can't corroborate or prove a story, I feel stories still have relevance.

Many of the episodes related in this book are just such evidence, experiences graciously relayed by those who experienced them. I've included a few of the more remarkable stories in the book because they are similar to an investigation or because they sharply contrast. And because, gosh darn it, who doesn't like a good ghost story?

PART I

INVESTIGATIONS

CHAPTER 1
A FAMILY AFFAIR

Middletown, Delaware

Our team had the honor to investigate a family-owned company with deep roots in Middletown, Delaware. Danny Burris is the owner and operator of PHB Inc. General Contractors, which specializes in home and light commercial projects. The company also boasts an on-site millwork shop that produces custom cabinetry and moldings. The Burris family has deep ties with the company going back to 1963, when Danny's father, C. C. "Toby" Burris, began working for Phillips Home Builders. The name changed in 1993, when the Burris family took over the operation. According to Danny, when his father first started working for Mr. Phillips, there was very little to the operation. Danny's office was Mr. Phillips's originally, and, aside from a back storage room, that was all that the building entailed.

PHB Inc. now encompasses a sprawling compound with several buildings and a fenced-in lot. The original PHB structure has been enlarged and added onto several times. Danny recalled how it all began.

"Dad came to work for Phillips in '63 and then in '72 we got into making furniture and millwork. And Mom and Dad built this [onto the existing structure] for storage. We repaired furniture, sold furniture. So my family built this," Danny said humbly, waving his arm at the larger open building outside his office.

The exterior of PHB Inc.

What the family created from old barn wood and scraps and pieces of torn-down buildings is a remarkably unique open-concept structure with a showroom below and a full kitchen and meeting area on the second floor. Throughout the building are antique pieces they've found. Hung on every wall is a collection of old tools—old saws and hammers, files and hatchets. A collection of old barber chairs is sprinkled throughout. Large standing placards display pictures and drawings of past projects the company has completed, including majestic mansions overlooking the Chesapeake Bay and even a car dealership of glittering glass and metal. It's apparent that PHB isn't your typical throw-up-a-house-a-week construction company, despite Danny's self-effacing demeanor.

Truly unique, the building invites discovery. It's also quite obviously a labor of love and a second home to the Burris clan, all of whom had at one time worked for the company.

The Backstory

Brian, our investigator, conducted the original interview with Danny, recording it on videotape. When I listened to the tape, it quickly became apparent that, while prosperous and close, the Burris family had also seen their share of loss and tragedy. Both of Danny's parents had died, albeit of natural causes, but what was truly appalling was the number of fatal automobile accidents the family had endured. A brother, two coworkers, and a sister-in-law, a twenty-three-year-old mother of two, all died in auto accidents. If any family might have a lingering member or two, this seemed to be the one.

Danny decided to forgo the preliminaries and got straight to the point: there were strange things going on at his home and his business, and he wanted an investigation done. It turned out that he'd been contemplating such an action for a number of years and only just finally decided to pursue it.

He began his account by describing fairly typical activity. He reported hearing footsteps on the first floor and on the stairs. He noted also that sometimes people had reported smelling cigarette smoke in isolated areas of the building where no smoking was permitted. Both of Danny's parents had been smokers.

Sometimes the sounds of breathing or sighing were heard. And oddly loud sounds, like banging on the walls, were sometimes heard. Danny confessed that he'd never actually seen an apparition or a mist form, but from his office door (which has a view of the stairs going up to the second floor) he often heard the sound of footsteps. When he looked up at the sound, he also sometimes caught the flash of movement over the top step, as if legs were going by. He specified that he didn't actually see legs, but more a flash of movement. All these things are fairly typical of locations with paranormal activity.

But then Danny's story became more interesting. "It's a family business," Danny reiterated, suggesting that the ghostly activity is tied very closely to the company and the Burris clan. Indeed, Danny said it all began in 1997, on a tragic December morning, when his brother Dave and another employee, David Robinson (often referred to by his last name in order to lessen confusion), died together in a fatal automobile accident while heading out to a job site. Danny continued, "Everything that we're talking about started happening after that. It started *right* after that. At the time, my brother's office was upstairs, and my office was downstairs. Robinson's office was across the street in the millwork building. We started hearing noises or hearing things—upstairs, downstairs, and in the millwork building—and we'd always say, 'Oh, it's one of the Daves.'"

Danny was careful to point out that none of the activity ever felt malicious or sinister. Instead, the things that occurred to any number of employees or family members always seemed lighthearted or prankish in nature, which was in tune with the type of personality his brother Dave had possessed. "It's not harmful or hurtful. In fact, we [the office staff] all laughed about it."

"Maybe," Danny continued, "it's our rational minds making it this and this and this. But after Dave was killed, all these weird things started to happen. I came in one day and the intercom button was lit up on my phone." Danny said he tried several times to turn off the intercom button, pressing it futilely again and again. The intercom button stubbornly stayed lit. This was a problem because in intercom mode the phone couldn't be used to answer or make calls. Obviously, the intercom feature worked only with other phones in-house. So, to what phone was the intercom connected, Danny wondered? Upon checking the other phones throughout the buildings, Danny realized that the intercom buttons were also lit on what was Dave's phone in the office upstairs and on what had been Robinson's phone in the office across the street. None of the other phones in the building were lit. More aggravating, none of the three phones could be disconnected from the intercom.

"So, I called the phone company, and the guy came out and disconnected the system, reprogrammed it, and turned it back on. He did it probably four or five times." The phone repairman couldn't get the intercom feature to turn off either. Danny said that his phone appeared to be irrevocably tied to the phones of the two dead men in an endless conference. "We ended up getting a new phone system installed because those three phones were locked out with the intercom."

Danny admitted that the odd occurrences happened periodically and were not just specific to family members. All PHB's employees have at some point also experienced the odd things. Carol, an office employee, had told Danny just a few weeks prior that she had been alone in the building. Someone walked up the steps, and when they got to the top step, they exhaled. Carol said, "I came around the corner and found that there was nobody there."

Joe, whose office is on the ground floor, often reported to Danny that he heard strange noises when alone in the building as well. Joe reported hearing what sounded like two or three people upstairs walking or even running about. Invariably, when Joe investigated the sounds, he'd find no one in the building with him.

Danny's wife, Tina, recounted an eerie incident to Danny. One afternoon she had been standing near the front door of the building when a sheet of paper floated down from the second-floor office, seemingly out of nowhere. Upon picking up the piece of paper, she found that it was a note written by Dave. The note wasn't personal, just a few jotted notes about a work project, but seeing something written in his handwriting was rather unnerving. And how had it come to be in her hands?

The main building wasn't the only site of strange happenings. In the millwork building, where Robinson's office had been, April, an employee, also reported strange phenomena. Danny said, "We told the employees that you would be coming and would be filming. And one of the questions you asked was if there was any activity across the street, and we said no."

Apparently, that was when April refuted that claim. April recounted that the door to a closet would periodically open on its own. What was more interesting was that the door didn't just swing open, which could easily be explained by a faulty latch on the door or a vacuum of air when an outer door was opened. What was weird about the closet door, April said, was the fact that the door knob actually twisted before the door swung open. The apparently unflappable April had kept what she'd witnessed to herself. She'd been briefed about the odd occurrences at PHB Inc. and thus chalked it up as another day at the office.

Danny then recalled the day when the copier repairman, Joe, came to service their machine. Apparently, Joe had other skills beyond simply repairing office machines, because he'd only been in the building a few short minutes before he started asking some pointed questions about the building's unseen inhabitants.

Joe had walked in and said, "I'm here to service your copier."

"That's fine. It's right over there," Harry, an employee at the time, had replied.

Joe entered the room and started working on the machine. A few minutes later, he came back out to Harry and asked, "Are there other people here?"

Harry explained that there were two women working upstairs. Joe hesitantly admitted that he wasn't asking about other employees in the building. "I don't mean that," Joe said. "I work with the paranormal, and there's other people here."

"Oh yeah, there's other people here," Harry agreed.

"I could feel it as soon as I walked in the door," Joe admitted.

The episode came to Danny's attention. His interest piqued, Danny had conversations with Joe on a couple of occasions and fully intended to invite Joe out to the building for a reading. Somehow, he never got around to setting up the meeting. When Danny finally got serious about having Joe come out, he found out that Joe himself had passed away.

With an enormous grill out the back door and a full-sized kitchen and dining area on the second floor, it's easy to see that PHB would be a wonderful place for employees and guests to gather for a repast. Danny admitted that many a Friday afternoon had been spent in just such a way with employees and friends of the family. "I used to have happy hour here every Friday, and I'd cook for everybody." One Friday evening there were eight men gathered upstairs with Danny, enjoying barbecue and drinks. Everyone present heard the front door open and then close downstairs. Footsteps crossed the floor and eventually climbed the stairs. All the heads in the room turned to see what new guest had arrived. They waited for a long moment, anticipating…

"And no one was there," said Danny. Eddy, a friend of Danny's, apparently didn't share the opinion that phantom footsteps and doors opening and closing by themselves were all in good fun.

On this particular evening Eddy told Danny vehemently that he'd heard the front door open and close, as had the other guests, and he heard someone walking up the stairs. If that someone didn't arrive soon, Eddy told Danny, he was leaving the party, by the back door. Eddy did just that a few moments later. He's apparently abruptly departed the building two or three times since the fateful happy-hour episode.

Conversing with a friend in his first-floor office one afternoon, Danny was behind his desk, his friend in a chair facing the showroom with a view of the front door. Again the front door opened and closed on its own, and then they heard footsteps clearly crossing the floor. His friend was stymied. "Danny, no one came in."

"It's probably Dave. Don't worry about it," Danny had said to him.

They laughed about it, because that's how Dave was. Dave had been a prankster who loved to play jokes on people. "He and Robinson were happy-go-lucky people," Danny explained to Brian.

But playing pranks on people may not be the only reason Dave remained, Danny speculated. When he died, he left behind five children from two marriages. A teenage daughter from the first marriage took the death particularly hard. She hadn't been all that close to Dave, and then he died without a reconciliation. Danny admitted that his niece had gone through a very angry period. "She was in a bad way, bad time, bad whatever. She wasn't that close to her father. She went to the cemetery and turned his headstone over." Perhaps Dave felt compelled to linger because he felt he hadn't properly said goodbye to those he loved, made peace with a teenage daughter who felt he'd wronged her.

Dave may not be the only spirit to wander the building, Danny contended. "We had a young fellow from Hodgson Vo-Tech's drafting department working for us." The young man, Gabe, interned and later worked at PHB for a couple of years while finishing high school at Hodgson. He'd apparently had a real talent for drafting, winning awards for it at competitions. Eventually, he'd graduated high school and left for college in Rhode Island. He completed his first year of college and returned home in the spring.

One morning during Gabe's break, a horrific and baffling crashing sound shook the whole PHB building. Danny recounted that the sound was so unbelievably loud and so violent that they believed at the time that a vehicle had crashed into the structure. "Joe actually got up from his desk and ran outside to see what had happened. He found nothing." There was no car, no crash site, no visible damage, and no way to account for the horrific sound. The sound of the crash wasn't the only disturbance that day, either. For the rest of the day, employees reported hearing rattling and shaking sounds. The sounds of muffled voices could be detected just out of range. And something or someone could be heard moving about the building. Danny received the call later in the afternoon from Gabe's brother: the young man had died in a car crash that very morning. He'd had the accident at the exact time that the unaccountable sound had occurred. "After that, other things were abnormal, so we figured that maybe Gabe was now with us." At this point during the interview, Danny threw up his hands as if to say the more the merrier.

But then the tenor of the conversation changed. Danny suggested that Gabe might have considered PHB his home as well because "he'd had no parents."

"No, let me rephrase that. Gabe..." Danny stopped at this point, obviously emotional. For a few moments he paused, peering down at his desk, before he continued. "Gabe was a..." Danny looked away, again discomfited, eyes filled with tears. "I'm sorry," he said brusquely. Brian said nothing, letting Danny collect himself. "Gabe was a special guy," he concluded vaguely and then abruptly changed the topic back to his brother. A few minutes later, Danny again returned to the topic of Gabe.

Gabe's father had died in a motorcycle accident when Gabe was two years old. When Gabe was ten, his mother was also killed in a motorcycle accident while driving home from a funeral. "So Gabe was twelve, his older sister was eighteen, and his older brother was twenty." Gabe's older brother applied for custody of his younger brother and raised him from then on.

"Great kid, nice kid, smart kid. Good-looking boy. Smart, talented. He took number two in the county in [an] architectural drafting [competition]. Talented, talented fellow. Just as nice ... and he was everybody's friend, and just a happy-go-lucky, good guy... You know, when that accident happened and that noise happened, it just made [sense]. You don't question what the noise was because Gabe was killed that day and that was what the noise was. That's how we rationalize half the shit we encounter around here." Apparently, if Gabe had come to join the crowd at PHB Inc., he was more than welcome to stay.

The House

The paranormal activity didn't actually limit itself to the family business, Danny informed Brian. Intermittently since Dave's death, Danny and his family had started to experience paranormal phenomena in their home as well, much to his family's chagrin. While Danny took a cavalier approach to the paranormal activity, his wife, Tina, daughter, Michelle, and his mother-in-law, Janet, in particular, were not as pleased. Tina had been so unnerved by the happenings in her home that she would not allow the team in to investigate, fearing that an investigation might agitate the spirit or spirits and cause an increase of activity.

The building in question is not old. Danny described his home as "a brand-new house on a piece of farm dirt, built in 1996. After my brother Dave was killed, we started having things [occur] at the house. It was the same thing, noises..." Michelle, who had been a child at the time, appeared to take the brunt of the attention. "It seemed to hover around her," Danny explained. She was lying in bed one evening when a water bottle on her dresser started compressing and expanding as if unseen fingers had been squeezing it and then releasing, squeezing and releasing. There was a picture in Michelle's room that hung over her dresser. She heard a banging noise one day and went to investigate, only to find that the picture had come off the wall. It wasn't lying on the dresser but on the carpet. "It didn't fall down," asserted Danny, but fell out.

Michelle also had strange malfunctions with her computer, which would turn off and on by itself. And one day Michelle saw a white form or mist coalesce before her very eyes.

Tina has also witnessed such wispy mists. She told Danny that she'd seen the mist out of the corner of her eye one day as it quickly sailed by. Both Tina and Michelle also reported seeing movement out of their peripheral vision at times, for which they could not account.

In a later interview I conducted with the family, Tina admitted to also seeing orbs, a fairly rare phenomenon. She reported that it had only happened twice, once when she was a young girl and the second time only a week before I spoke with her. Tina described the ball of light as floating about the room with apparent purpose before it exited under her bedroom door. Tina immediately opened the door, which led out into the hall, but saw nothing more. The ball of light had simply vanished.

The human inhabitants weren't the only ones affected by the apparent phenomena. Tina noted that the family dogs would be walking down the hall in a straight path and then suddenly take a detour, as if moving around something that Tina couldn't see. Other times the dogs would be on the bed, intently staring at something—again, something only they could see. Then quite suddenly the dogs would catapult themselves off the bed and run pell-mell down the stairs as if being pursued.

Both of Danny's children are now grown and have moved away. When his son, Daniel, vacated his bedroom, it became a guest room in which Danny's mother-in-law, Janet, would sleep when she came for periodic visits. At least, Danny noted, that was where she used to stay. She found the nights spent in that room ran the gamut from mildly alarming to terrifying. "She said, 'There's something in the room, there's people in the room, and I can't be in there.' To this day she won't even walk into that room," Danny noted.

To be amenable to Janet's discomfort, Danny and his wife elected to put her up in his daughter's room. But that arrangement wasn't without its complications either. She had visited the family no more than two months before the interview, and in the week that she was there she reported distinctly feeling the bed shaking on two nights. Then one night as she was sleeping on her side, she felt the covers lift up behind her and then the depressing of the mattress as if someone had gotten into the bed with her. She lay there for a long moment in terror. When she finally got up the nerve to look behind her, she saw no one there. She related that moment of terror to Danny, recounting that she'd literally been too frightened to even scream. "I was going to scream," she said, "but I had no breath to scream."

Janet came again the weekend before the interview, and, according to Danny, she came downstairs on Sunday morning with a new tale of the macabre.

She asked Tina, "Why did you move the bed?"

"What do you mean?" Tina asked.

"The entire bed has been moved," Janet said.

Upon inspection of the bed, Danny and Tina had to agree with Janet: the evidence was irrefutable that something or someone had moved the bed. The markings in the carpet where the feet of the bed had been compared to the location the bed was now in indicated a move of around three inches, by Danny's estimation. "It's a big bed, and you couldn't just bump it and move it." Tina stoutly refuted moving it either. When she visits, Janet now sleeps on the couch downstairs, where for some reason she isn't disturbed.

Danny recalled that workmen called to the home were not immune to pranks by the unseen. The whirlpool tub in the master suite had failed, and he was having a new one installed by members of his own staff. "Twice one morning I had guys in the bathroom when the fan came on . . . by itself," he said. Danny clarified that at least one of the workmen witnessed the switch to the fan actually flip up by itself. Just the day before the interview, another workman had been finishing the job when the fan came on again. "He turned around and asked my son, Daniel, if he had flipped the switch and Daniel said, 'No, I didn't touch anything.'"

Danny's daughter, Michelle, has set up and now runs a beauty salon on the second floor of the family's detached garage building. Tina was in the kitchen one day talking to Daniel when his sister called from the salon and directed him to come up immediately. He came upstairs and asked her why he was there, and she directed him to be quiet and listen. They both distinctly heard a violin playing. The violin music was loud enough that the women having their hair done also heard it and commented on it. Danny reported that his grandmother had played violin and that he still had her instrument.

Between the initial interview with the Burris family and the actual investigation, I came home one night and found a text from Danny with a video attachment. Alone in her salon, Michelle had once again heard music and been able to record it on her phone. On the short recording there was an audible sound of some type of musical instrument that sounded very much like a harmonica.

Traveling Cigarette Smoke

During Brian's interview, Danny brought up a new phenomenon that wasn't tied to any specific location but appeared to follow him around. He admitted that he often smelled cigarette smoke in the unlikeliest places. Sometimes he smelled smoke while at the office, in a building where it is forbidden to smoke. He'd also smelled it at other locations. He had smelled it while attending a church service. Sometimes he'd smelled it at his house, though neither he nor Tina smoke. "I've been all different places and smelled it," he concluded. He admitted that both of his parents had smoked, and he often caught the smell in unusual places, and invariably it would remind him of them. Olfactory phenomena are not at all unusual in hauntings, as a distinctive scent is immediately evocative of a person, our scents being extremely personal. If a person had worn a certain cologne, smoked cigars, or had a scent that was unique to them, it serves as a calling card to announce their presence. It seems as if this particular calling card was left for Danny to remind him that his parents were often close.

Dave's Former Residence

Dave had owned a house a block over from the office. It was sold after his death to a man who moved into it with his daughter. One day the new owner came by the office to deliver a box of Dave's old papers and also brought a message for Danny. It seemed that, while

Dave had departed and the house was sold, Dave himself hadn't gotten the eviction notice. Even before the final purchase of the house, the next-door neighbor had told the new owner that he had sometimes spotted Dave staring out a window of his former home.

Once residing in the house, the new owner started sensing Dave's fatherly presence. Dave, who had left behind five children of his own, now watched over the homeowner's daughter, helpfully shutting doors she left open or turning off lights she left on.

"Yeah, he looks over my daughter," the man said. "You can't believe. He'll close the door and make sure she's okay. And we talk to him …" Deciding to test his theory, the homeowner performed an experiment. He asked the entity, "If you're here, turn the light switch on." Apparently, the light switch flipped on. It convinced him that all these things weren't just merely coincidences after all.

Can an entity haunt more than one location? It certainly makes sense that Dave, perhaps not knowing he's dead or perhaps not knowing what else to do, is performing the same routine he did while he was living. He goes to work during the day and travels home at night. And then occasionally he may go out to Danny's place with the intention of scaring Janet, a woman Danny admitted Dave loved to tease when he was living.

The activity at the office coupled with the carefully orchestrated harassment of Janet and the activity reported at Dave's former residence all appeared to strongly suggest that his brother Dave was trying very hard to inform his family of his continued presence. I was hoping that the results of the investigation would prove that point.

The Investigation

We arrived at PHB with a full cast of characters, seven in total. Maya, Renne, Gene, and I had been on numerous investigations in the past, but with us were three new recruits, Brianna, Karl, and Sarah. I was hoping it would be a good investigation to also conduct some training. We set up at the facility, running surveillance cameras on the main floor, the staircase (where Danny had reported seeing what he described as legs moving up the stairs), and a wide angle of the second story. We also had handheld video cameras and audio recorders placed strategically around the building. On the second floor and main floor, we honestly recorded nothing of note. In the office space, which is part of the original building, we did record a couple of relatively strong EVPs.

As I said before, I brought a team of seven investigators, thinking the building large enough to accommodate the numbers. I quickly regretted that decision. All the old planks and boards that Danny had salvaged and that lent such a lovely patina to the building quickly proved to be a sound hazard. A team upstairs that moved even minimally would cause creaking and squeaking floorboards that resounded throughout the rest of the building. The same could be said for the first floor. Anytime any person moved the entire building reverberated with the noise. Evidence review became a misery of *creak, creak, creak, groan*.

This might, obviously, be a contributor to the sounds of footsteps that the owner reported hearing over and over. Could the wood settling and moving in different weather conditions and humidity be causing what sounded like footsteps coming in the door and moving up the staircase? Certainly, it couldn't be ruled out.

Audio recorders in the older part of the building seemed to have caught the clearest evidence. One EVP we caught was a male voice that responded to our request for its name. Of course, in the way of things, he didn't actually answer us with his name but instead offered a noncommittal "Do it."

In the probable highlight of the evening, the team composed of Renne, Brianna, and Karl was able to interact, using EMF detectors, with a seemingly unseen participant. These exchanges are fairly rare but always welcome when they occur. The investigators asked a number of yes/no questions, and the entity was able to answer in the positive by lighting up one or more of the detectors and seemed to move about from one detector to another. It wasn't a surprise that the conversation was focused on building construction when the positive responses began. The team did an excellent job of connecting with the spirit by speaking his own language.

Below is a portion of that transcript recorded on the first floor of PHB Inc. that evening. It should be noted that each team member had an EMF detector with them during the exchange, either in their hands or placed in various locations nearby, and that more than one device responded throughout.

RENNE: We are downstairs in Middletown, Delaware, at the architect's office.[3] Do we have anyone down here? We seemed to have someone upstairs.

BRIANNA: It's so creaky in here. (*A couple of creaks are heard as Brianna moves furtively around the room.*) There is no being quiet in here. If someone's here, can you make the meter flicker? (*The lights flicker on the EMF detector in Brianna's hand.*) Thank you. Can you do that again?

KARL: (*To Brianna*) Did it make your meter flicker?

---

3. I'm not sure why Renne assumed that the company was an architectural firm. However, I do tend to keep the details of cases pretty close to the vest. I don't want the team to go in, especially those who feel themselves to be more sensitive, with preconceived notions.

Suddenly the team's attention was piqued. It had been a fairly non-eventful evening up to then.

Brianna: Yes. Can you make it flicker one more time? Please...

Renne: If you're here, did you work as an architect?

Renne: Are you an apprentice? Or are you maybe attached to the objects in the room, like a barber chair? Or one of the old tools? Can you tell us your name?

Brianna: Can you tell us how you passed away?

Renne: How old are you?

Long pause. The team slowly assembles as a group near the center of the room.

Brianna: Upstairs there seemed to be someone playing with my lights. They seemed to really like the lights (*referring to her handheld EMF detector*). Do you want to make them flicker? (*To the team*) Did you see that? (*To the room*) Can you make them flicker again?

Karl: I'm getting a strong EMF spike.

Karl's meter also starts flickering.

Brianna: Thank you. Do you like the lights?

Karl: Can you do that again, please?

Brianna: Can you bring it to a yellow, please?[4]

---

4. On the meter, different colored lights signify higher levels of EMF. Green lights indicate the lower range of 1.5 to 2.5 milligauss, yellow signifies the middle range of 5 to 10 mG, orange indicates 10 to 20 mG, and red is 20 or more mG.

KARL: It's trying.

KARL AND BRIANNA: Thank you.

Apparently, one of the meters lights up all the way to yellow. The meter had shot up quite forcefully.

KARL: Wow, thank you. That took a lot of energy to do that.

BRIANNA: Can you make my meter go to yellow, please?

RENNE: Is this the same person who was upstairs, or is this another person?

KARL: All right, thank you.

KARL: (*Whispering*) It's cold right here. Do you feel that?

RENNE: I do, actually.

BRIANNA: It's cold on the left side of my left leg.

RENNE: It's my feet. My feet and my ankles [are cold].

KARL: Yeah, mine too. And the back of my neck. It feels like it's breathing on me.

KARL: Right here (*indicating where he's feeling the cold on his leg*).

BRIANNA: That's where mine is (*rubbing her left leg*).

KARL: Is that you?

BRIANNA: Did you come down to be with us and talk to us?

KARL: Are you with us right now?

RENNE: Can you stomp on the floor? Jiggle a doorknob?

There is a creaking noise overhead.

RENNE: That's upstairs.

KARL: Did you hear that?

RENNE: It's upstairs. They're walking.

BRIANNA: Can you hold it on yellow please?

KARL: It just did it.

RENNE AND BRIANNA: Thank you.

RENNE: Can you show us in some way that you're here? Like whoever upstairs did. If you're the same person, can you pull? Pull our pants legs or…

KARL: Move my hat.

RENNE: Pull my hair or touch my shoulder?

A pause of several seconds occurs.

RENNE: You have all these people walking around. Do you like all these people? Do you feel like you're at work again? You can tell us to get out. Tell us in that little recorder over there. Tell us to get out.

A pause of a few seconds occurs, and then one of the meters lights up.

KARL: Wow.

RENNE: Thanks for lighting that up.

KARL: It really lit up when you said that.

There is a pause of a few seconds, during which creaks are heard from the floor above.

RENNE: That was up above. You cannot walk up there without the floor squeaking, creaking.

BRIANNA: You're right, there's no way. (*Pause*) Is your name Gabriel? Or Gabe?[5] My friend had a home improvement company like twenty years ago.[6]

RENNE: That's all right. You still know more than we do. I worked for a builder for a few years and I still ... (*Addressing the spirit*) When you build these houses, what type of insulation do you use? What's the R factor?

BRIANNA: Karl was raised around construction. So you may have that in common. Can you light up his meter, please?

KARL: It just went to yellow.

BRIANNA: It went to yellow?

KARL: Yeah.

BRIANNA: Can you do that again please?

KARL AND BRIANNA: Thank you.

KARL: I grew up on job sites. Did you? It went up a little bit. Yeah.

RENNE: I used to work for a builder. I used to order the insulation and the lighting.

KARL: It's going ... nuts.

---

5. I hadn't told the team about the possible connection with Gabe, but Brianna had unwittingly read his obituary, which was prominently mounted in a frame on the wall on the second floor.

6. Brianna is trying to explain her lack of knowledge of the building industry. One of the best things to do to encourage activity is find a common bond with an entity. If they were in the construction business, you talk construction. If it's a child, you tell them a story, and so on. I've often found that when I have managed to make that connection, my success is far greater, the evidence of better quality.

RENNE: The Dryvit, the siding. That's what they used to use.

KARL: Yeah.

RENNE: That was back in the nineties.

KARL: Yeah.

BRIANNA: I've got a chill going up and down my shoulder. (*Whispering in excitement*) This is so great.

RENNE: I used to get the Dryvit, and there was something else. There was another one they had besides Dryvit, and I can't remember what it was called.

KARL: It was a synthetic stucco. It lit up when I said that. Like it knew.

RENNE: Typar, I used to order the Typar and the Tyvek.

KARL: (*Laughing*) Yeah, when I said that it went…(*Indicates the meter going up and down with a hand motion.*)

RENNE: I remember the builder I worked for. He had to pour the foundations and make them waterproof.

KARL: Wow. Did you see? (*Meter goes off again.*)

RENNE: Did you have to do that? Was that all part of your architectural plans?

KARL: Wow.

Notice how many more EMF spikes occurred when the team started talking about building materials. Materials would have been something that, as a builder, Dave would have dealt with every day. Case in point: I was in the dentist's office having some work done recently, and as I sat in the chair incapacitated, the dentist and his enthusiastic young assistant talked animatedly about the pros and cons of dental supplies for what felt like a small eternity. We are our careers, the work we do, and the labor we train for and we take pride in. I credit the success of the EMF conversation to the crew, who did a good job of tapping into that.

The Evidence

This is an excerpt from the evidence log of the EMF exchange between Renne, Karl, and Brianna. Renne's audio recorder was stationed on the first floor in the main business area. The time denotes hours and minutes.

2:03 Brianna reports a KII spike.

2:03 Karl's KII meter spikes to a yellow.

2:06 KII spike to yellow on stationary KII.

2:07 Group reports feeling cold around the feet and ankles, later around the neck and shoulders.

2:08 KII spike into yellow stationary KII.

2:10 KII spike to yellow, and then again immediately after stationary KII.

2:12 KII spike.

2:13 KII spike.

2:38	Karl's KII spikes to yellow.
2:39	Mel Meter EMF stationed by stairs chirped.
2:45	Indistinguishable whisper recorded.
2:46:09	KII hit.
2:46:41	KII hit.

The amount of evidence the team collected was not outstanding. While the EMF session was interesting, I wouldn't consider it conclusive. I would have liked an accompanying EVP or moving shadow caught on film to help confirm that something had been truly going on.

I interpreted the one clear EVP caught that night, the male saying "Do it" in answer to our request that he tell us his name, as an entity convincing himself to tell us his name. Sadly, he didn't.

Contamination, my old nemesis, was an issue. Even the smallest movements by the team caused the floorboards to creak loudly. I listened to hours of creaking, groaning, squeaking, squealing floors until I peeled the headphones off in disgust. It made me wonder, what might we have caught if not for the contamination?

Final Assessment

The frustrating truth about investigating is that if the activity is of a residual nature, it will only happen when the environmental factors are right. If it's an intelligent haunting and it's avoiding you, then you may get nothing as well. And of course the third alternative, one that should be carefully considered, is that the so-called activity has a natural explanation. Certainly, reports of footsteps in this particular building with its creaking floors were suspect. Multiple people, all fully awake, hearing the front door opening and closing followed by footsteps moving across the floor and up the stairs—well, that's another story.

My gut feeling was (though I'd like far more evidence to prove it) that Brother Dave haunted PHB Inc., sometimes went home to his place of residence, and sometimes traveled out to Danny's house to harass Janet. Why? It may very well be the fact that his death was abrupt. He was in a work truck going out to a job site one moment and dead in another. It may be that Dave had no idea what happened and therefore wasn't aware of the fact that he's now deceased.

Then again, it may be that Dave had too much unfinished business. He died leaving behind five children of various ages, a family business, brothers, a wife... Perhaps he simply couldn't let go. When a person has a wasting disease, they have time to become accustomed to the fact that their time is limited. They have time to say goodbyes and square up, for example, with an angry adolescent daughter with whom they'd had a misunderstanding. That isn't the case when death meets us unexpectedly.

The reason I suggested it was Dave and not one of the others was that the activity seemed mischievous and good-natured, which matched his characteristic tendencies as described in his own brother's accounts. His fatherly inclinations toward the young girl who now lived in his house seemed to affirm his parental leanings.

Gabe, I speculated, was more of what we would consider a crisis apparition. Crisis apparitions occur directly at the time of death or very soon after. It is the departed's way of signaling that something terrible just happened. I speculated that if they had noted the time of the horrible sound of a vehicle smashing (supposedly into the building), that sound that sent Joe racing out of the building, they would have found that it correlated exactly with the moment that the fatal accident occurred.

That is the way that crisis apparitions work. It is in effect a telepathic distress call to the living that something horrible just happened, something that needs immediate attention. The fact that Danny had mentored, probably fathered in many ways, the young man and that they shared a deep emotional attachment was obvious. We can't always choose our family... but then sometimes we can. I've already mentioned the fact that the young man's obituary is framed and hung prominently on the wall on the second floor of the building—so prominently that one of my investigators found it, read it, and included it in an EVP session without any prior knowledge of the situation. That spoke volumes. The oral disturbances that followed the rest of the day, I speculate, were Gabe's way of trying to communicate with Danny about the tragedy.

The cigarette smoke that seemed to follow Danny around to various odd locations may just be annoying people with a cigarette habit. Or it could be a form of after-death communication (ADC). ADCs are a type of phenomenon that happen when deceased family members attempt to communicate with living loved ones. They do not constitute conventional hauntings but are short visits of our departed loved ones in essence checking in to say, "I'm okay. How are you?"

These phenomena can take various forms, from oddly lucid dreams, to familiar symbols, to feelings like a person is being touched or even embraced. Olfactory phenomena are extremely powerful. Our sense of smell is connected to the oldest part of the brain, the amygdala, or primal brain stem. Thus, a smell can elicit an immediate sympathetic response.

Case in point: I was swapping stories with a painter at her art studio in Beaufort, South Carolina, one lovely afternoon. In the course of our conversation, she informed me that she had been at home one evening when she had unmistakably smelled the scent of her grandmother's perfume. She was alone, sitting on a couch, when this overwhelming scent caught her attention. The power of the scent and the fact that its presence could not be accounted for in an empty room left her so unnerved that she ran out of the house. She spoke about the incident later with her sister, who admitted that she had had a similar experience. Grandmother, apparently, was checking up on her granddaughters.

The fact that Danny smelled the very distinctive smell of cigarette smoke, a scent clearly connected with both his parents, seems to indicate that one or the other was checking in. This was a very closely connected clan, a family that was running a multigenerational company, a business that connected both parents and four brothers—truly a family not to be separated from one another even by the gulf of death.

Postscript

As I said before, the evidence we caught wasn't terribly illuminating, and it left many questions unanswered. Honestly, I would have liked to have returned to do another investigation. It's wonderful when we get the chance to do multiple investigations at one location. With multiple investigations, the evidence yield has the potential to grow. However, after our investigation wrapped, Danny and his family instead solicited the help of an area psychic. During her reading of the building, according to Danny, she said that she had connected with the spirit of Dave. She said he was something of a smart aleck who liked to tease people. And she brought up several details that Danny confirmed only Dave could have known. Apparently, the topic of feral cats was one such detail that convinced Danny she had actually made contact with his deceased brother.

Danny relayed the story to me. His mother had started feeding a few feral cats that were roaming about the property. The promise of a free meal was trumpeted around the neighborhood, and the number of homeless cats quickly grew to twenty-five. Realizing that they had a problem, the family contacted a cat rescue group who came and crated up twenty-four of them; the last cat evaded capture. They took all the cats to a vet, who performed twenty-four sterilization operations. Then the group brought all twenty-four feral cats back to the Burrises. Finally, a friend of the family who owned a farm with a mouse infestation agreed to take the cats. All twenty-five feral cats were caught, crated, and moved to a new home. According to the psychic, Dave was recalling this comic episode in their shared lives.

I interviewed Danny a final time when I was gathering information for this book. He confirmed that the paranormal activity continued unabated at both the business and the house. Just that weekend, Tina's two-year-old great-nephew had been at the house for a family get-together. He started climbing the stairs, which is dangerous for one so young. Everyone present had implored the boy to stop, which he did when he reached the landing. He had turned around and looked back down the stairs when his mother called to him. But before she could run up the steps and scoop him to safety, he turned back around to face the second floor and began waving as if at a person. When the boy's mother arrived, she looked up the stairs to see who the child was waving to but saw only an empty hallway. The child's behavior had been so strange that everyone at the get-together had discussed it at some length. Obviously, the child had been going up the stairs to meet someone, the same someone he had greeted with a little-boy wave. But who had he seen?

CHAPTER 2
LITTLE HOUSE IN THE WOODS

Hartly, Delaware

Nestled on a wooded lot, the little cedar-shake house in Hartly, Delaware, hardly fits our picture of a haunted house. But if there's one thing I've found about the paranormal, it's that it rarely fits the Hollywood picture. In the previous chapter, I commented that it is always desirable to do multiple investigations of a property in order to establish a broader evidence base from which to work. This little house in the woods is the perfect case in point.

I've had the pleasure of working with homeowners Lindsey and Aaron for four years now. I performed not only three investigations at their home but also two investigations at a property where Aaron was the general contractor. By the way, both of the properties in question were undergoing major renovations, which often leads to an increase in paranormal activity. It's such a prevalent factor in hauntings that it's one of the first questions I ask during my initial interviews with prospective clients. If we believe that entities have some intelligence, a reaction to the commotion would probably not be surprising. They see the structure as their home, and suddenly some stranger is tearing out walls and breaking up the floor.

The exterior of the house.

When the team started to look into the history of the home and its former owner or owners, we found that the whole situation was rather unique. The former owner of the property was Phillip Goldberg, who turned out to be a rather astounding figure for backwater Hartly. He'd attended an Ivy League university but had left before graduating to run his family's business, steering them through the turbulent years of the Great Depression. He had done a tour of duty during World War II and had been awarded several medals for bravery.

After the war, he returned to college, eventually completing a PhD, and ended his career as a professor at various local colleges. Among his many pursuits, he'd also been trained in hypnotherapy.

At some point he acquired a large piece of land. Always the entrepreneur, Goldberg had divided the larger property into smaller lots along a backcountry road and then moved (instead of building) small existing houses onto the lots as rental units.

Lindsey and Aaron's home had actually been two houses moved there and placed via crane in 1953. The two separate buildings were connected, end to end, making the structure feel somewhat like a jigsaw puzzle. One building appeared to have been a very small 1940s-era two-story home, with one bedroom in the loft area. The second building was a one-story building bearing few architectural details, which made the age of the building hard to determine. Because of the odd connection, the long central hallway had a decided jag in the middle. Doors opened to the outside in odd places. There were in essence two front doors, neither of which faced the road, but a side door off the bedroom hallway did. A small closet that probably started its life as a hallway closet had one opening into the hall and another to the rear of the closet that opened into the master bedroom.

Neither the owners nor the team have been able to ascertain where the two homes had originally stood or who had owned them, making the origin of the haunting even more of a mystery. Did the ghost or ghosts come with one or both of the houses? Was it something that resided on the land and had since taken up residence in the home after the buildings were placed there? We simply do not know.

As county records and title searches only establish owners of a property, and not renters, we were also not able to establish who had rented the home throughout the years. What we were able to establish was that the Goldberg family never lived in the building but had owned a larger home up the road. Goldberg's wife was killed in an accident in her seventies, and Goldberg followed her a couple years later from natural causes. The couple left behind two grown children. Presumably desiring to cash in on their inheritance, the family placed the rental properties up for sale. The housing market being stale at the time, many of the houses did not sell for years. In fact, the house next door to Lindsey and Aaron's was still vacant when last I visited. Their house stood empty for eight years before the enterprising young couple decided to take on the project of bringing it back from the brink. Seeing it as a quiet place to raise their children, they made an offer and closed on the property in 2012. Aaron, a contractor by trade, wasn't deterred by the ramshackle condition of the house, though the building was in very rough shape, and started making repairs immediately. Unfortunately, he worked long hours running his own construction business and was often gone, leaving the repairs unfinished. Indeed, Lindsey recalled a time early on when there was a gaping hole in the dining room floor that she attempted to keep her toddler daughter from falling into.

Certainly, the first two or three years must have been difficult for the couple, with Aaron gone on jobs and Lindsey home alone in the old building with her young daughter and later an infant son. It also rather quickly became plain, at least to Lindsey, that there were others residing in the home as well, residents who were not necessarily visible but were making their occupancy clear in rather remarkable ways. In the beginning, the strange things that happened appeared to be benign. But as the renovations began in earnest, the activity seemed to both increase and change in tenor until one fateful night when Lindsey saw something that changed her mind about the friendly nature of her unseen guests and set her on the path to seeking help. She also found the information about Goldberg during her search on the history of the property. She found his background in hypnotherapy extremely interesting.

Who better to haunt a building than someone trained in hypnotherapy? she wondered. I surmised that Lindsey equated hypnosis with ESP as ways to tap into a person's unconscious mind. While I've often been skeptical of the idea that the Goldbergs, or Mrs. Goldberg in particular, haunted the property, Lindsey remains steadfast in her conviction that such is the case. In fact, in a recent email to me, she recounted the Goldberg's daughter had stopped by the house to discuss some business with Aaron. While there, she was playing with the children. Lindsey recounted that she began feeling an overwhelming sense of happiness and peace in the house, which strengthened her conviction about the identity of their unseen inhabitant.

I tell all my clients when they first contact us for an investigation to establish a log of events to keep details straight, as human memory is a fickle thing at best. Of course, by the time my organization is contacted, a family may have been experiencing anomalous events for a number of years. It then becomes a guessing game about whether they witnessed the dark shadow in the hallway before or after they heard the ghostly piano music on the baby monitor. This is the case with the Hartly house, as the family had been living in the house two years before they contacted me. Thus, it's difficult to impossible at this point to establish a perfect timeline of events. What I've tried to do instead is link like evidence with like and build to the crescendo that finally convinced Lindsey to seek outside help.

The Backstory

It started, as these things often do, with electrical disturbances. The fact that lights would flicker on and off was perhaps not surprising for an old house with old wiring. Radios and TVs would also flicker or change stations. Aaron was slowly replacing worn fixtures and worn wiring to correct the problem, to no avail. The electrical malfunctions had continued. On our third investigation, Lindsey described strange TV behavior. One evening she woke up to find the program playing on their bedroom TV in fast-forward, though their cable device did not have this functionality. Wondering if there was a problem with the cable service, she went into the family room to look at the TV there. In the family room the program was playing at the proper speed. Now she was confused. How could programs on cable run at different speeds on different TVs? A trip back to the bedroom confirmed it: the TV in the bedroom was still playing at a different speed.

TVs in the home had a history of mystifying misbehavior, apparently. Aaron recalled a day when his son was in the family room watching snow on the TV. Very young at the time, Romeo appeared to be communicating with something in the room, waving his hands and jabbering away in baby talk. Watching from the porch, Aaron witnessed his son babbling happily as he watched nothing on the TV. What happened next had Aaron perplexed. A confounded Aaron watched the TV change from snow to a cartoon with no one touching the remote. Had Romeo been communicating with an unseen spirit, imploring him or her to change the channel?

Lindsey also noted that the family would often hear strange banging or crashing noises, but upon investigation of the sound, they would find nothing out of place. Lindsey also said she had sometimes seen a shadowy mass moving in the hallway as she was lying in bed looking into the bureau mirror across the room. Then too there was the odd shadow that they caught out of the corner of their eye when watching the family room TV. This TV hangs on the stairway wall. This same wall has a square cutout so that someone sitting on the couch facing the TV can see across the staircase and into the dining room. In the same corner, visible from the couch is a wood-burning stove that the family installed. On many evenings, Aaron or Lindsey would see a shadowy figure moving about by the wood-burning stove in what Lindsey described as a pattern-like motion. In other words, the figure would always be seen moving in the same direction, moving from the center of the room and heading toward the wall. Speculating that this might be residual activity, I examined the wall, thinking I might find evidence that there had been a door there once. I did not find evidence of that, however, as the window in the wall appears to be original to the structure.

On the team's first investigation of the property, we caught a strange mist in that area that appeared in one photo but was gone by the next. All the doors and windows were closed at the time, it being winter. We didn't see the mist with our eyes, so it didn't become apparent until we were in evidence review. We had taken multiple photos of the same area since and had never been able to re-create an image with a mist.

But strange mists are not out of the ordinary at the Hartly house. An odd mist was reported by a visitor to the house who was unaware of the house's haunted reputation. He had entered the bathroom one day when he came face to manifestation with a strange fog simply hanging in the air. No one had showered recently, and the entire room wasn't fogged—just a small dense area had this foggy mist. It was so odd that the visitor reported it to Lindsey and Aaron.

Lindsey also noted that she herself had witnessed in her hallway closet what she described as a substance that looked like waves of heat rising from a hot road. This shimmery heat-wave substance appeared to be floating in her closet at eye level. She had seen the same substance on the video feed off Romeo's baby monitor in the past. She noted one night that Romeo appeared to be interacting with the heat waves and at one point appeared to part the cloud with his hand.

More recently, Aaron had started seeing a small, shadowy figure by the kitchen when he was in the family room. The figure was small like a child. The first time it happened, Aaron thought he'd caught his daughter in the act of sneaking out of bed. He didn't find her in the kitchen when he investigated, and a trip down the hall proved that she was in bed asleep as she should have been. He's since witnessed this small apparition multiple times.

Then one fateful night, Lindsey awoke to a truly terrifying sight. Standing in the doorway of the hallway closet (recall that the back of the closet opens to the master bedroom) and seemingly gazing in at her was the dark figure of a man. He stood there for some time as Lindsey lay there too frightened to make a sound. It was as if the figure wanted Lindsey to see him, as if he wanted her to know that he was there watching her, spying on her, passing judgment. The figure finally faded away, but her terror remained. She began researching the property the very next day. When asked, she admitted that they had been in the middle of refurbishing the bathroom across the hall from their bedroom when this sighting occurred.

Lindsey isn't the only one to have witnessed the dark, male figure. A visitor to her house also saw him, unwittingly. Lindsey wrote in an email to me, "We had a friend of ours just last week who had no background knowledge about our energy here. He said that he was walking down the hallway to use the restroom when he saw a shadow in the shape of a human figure that walked into our master bedroom through the hallway closet. He came back and told us, and he had been pretty shaken up." The fact that the friend had no knowledge that the house was haunted, and therefore no preconceived notions, made this account stronger from an evidential standpoint. One doesn't expect to go to a friend's house, turn the corner, and see an unexplained shadowy figure walking into a room.

When Lindsey first contacted me, she told me quite plainly that she sensed there were two entities in the house, a male and a female. The male entity was more standoffish, while the female was more interactive, perhaps even downright friendly. Lindsey recalled a day when she was in the kitchen and she and Aaron were having a heated discussion. The argument was building in volume when suddenly Lindsay felt a push on her shoulder, a shove that literally propelled her out of the kitchen. "All right," Lindsey had said, "Apparently you don't want me in there." The preternatural push did what it had been intended to do: break up the discussion.

Aside from diffusing marital disputes, the female entity appeared to have adopted the role of family protector as well, a role that has saved the family at least twice from house fires. In an email sent to me, Lindsey wrote that she had awoken out of a sound sleep one night and smelled smoke. The smell was so strong she got out of bed to check the house but found no source for the odor. Lindsey felt that the smell of fire where no fire could be found was precognitive of the two events that happened shortly after.

The first incident started benignly enough. Lindsey wandered out to the wood-floored attached porch one day and realized a rug on the floor would be nice. She had just the thing, she recalled: an old rug of her mother's that she had stored in the back storage room. One of these days, she thought, she'd have to find it and try it out there. Throughout the rest of the day, at odd times Lindsey would find herself thinking again about the old rug. Thoughts of that rug kept creeping into her head at the oddest moments. She just couldn't stop thinking about that rug. Finally, she gave into the pressure and went to find the rug. When she got to the storage room, she had an unexpected revelation. An overheated lamp had fallen onto the rug and had left a singed spot. If she hadn't found it then, it very likely would have started a fire. Had the female spirit been trying to communicate the danger to her telepathically all day long?

And fire was the theme in another bizarre episode. One evening Lindsey had gone out to greet Aaron, who was coming home from work. While standing at the truck door conversing with him, she happened to glance into the side-door mirror. Reflected in the mirror was a sight that left Lindsey in a panic. She quite clearly saw flames. The flames were so shockingly real in fact, that she spun around to look at the front of the house, specifically at the chimney, to see if her house was ablaze. She saw nothing. However, now somewhat in a panic, she ran into and through the house to the attached porch on the other side. On the porch she found the ashtray ablaze. In our initial interview, Lindsey concluded, "There was no way his truck could have shown a reflection of the porch, but something made me run out there to check on it, and if that didn't happen, we would've had a fire."

One of the characteristics that makes Lindsey one of my favorite clients is the fact that she's so down-to-earth about the odd things that happen in her home. She's not calling in a priest and sprinkling holy water every time something weird happens. She's more interested in knowing what is going on.

The family's daughter, Savanna, hasn't had a lot of encounters with the spirits. She did tell her mother once that she had seen a woman outside her bedroom window. And once while we were there for an evidence reveal, the girl admitted to me that she heard things out in the hallway sometimes. But in retrospect, Savanna appeared to have the least contact with the spirits of the house. That is not the case, however, with the couple's son, Romeo.

From the start, the little boy seemed to have caught the interest of our female spirit. Toddlers and infants often keep odd sleeping habits, but Romeo's were odder than most. He would be up until all hours of the night babbling in his room. He seemed to be interacting with someone or something that only he could see. And Lindsey and Aaron reported that they sometimes would hear piano music on the monitor. In the house was a piano that Lindsey's mother had painstakingly scrimped and saved for. This heirloom instrument had originally been purchased for her son when he was a child, but Lindsey had inherited it when her mother passed away. It stood by one of the front doors at the other end of the hallway from Romeo's room. Nowhere near Romeo's room stood the piano, and yet the two bewildered parents would hear piano music when it was impossible for there to be anyone playing it. And I've already mentioned the heatwave anomaly Lindsey and Aaron sometimes witnessed on the baby monitor hanging over the crib in Romeo's room.

While the house has been investigated four times, the first investigation was performed by another area group. That team performed a quick two-hour investigation while Aaron and Lindsey sat out on the porch. The investigation netted a couple of EVPs, which, while not an astounding amount of evidence, was enough to pique Lindsey's interest. She contacted me shortly after the initial investigation to ask me to perform another.

It should be noted that, while Lindsey believed early on that the house was haunted, it took longer for the skeptical Aaron to accept that there was something odd about the building. The faulty wiring and the thumps and bumps he could rationally argue away. He also didn't spend as much time in the home as did Lindsey. Aaron told me that it wasn't until the night of the first paranormal investigation that he actually accepted that certain things that happened in the house had no rational explanation.

The very first time the couple had their house investigated by a paranormal team, they put Romeo to sleep and then waited close by on the porch, listening while the team did their sweep. The group then gathered their gear and left, and Lindsey and Aaron went back inside. Before turning in himself, Aaron headed to the children's rooms to check that they were sleeping. When he got to Romeo's room, he was befuddled to find that something was barring his entrance into the room. At first he couldn't figure out what. The door itself wasn't locked, yet when he pushed on the door, it would only open a couple of inches. When he knelt down and examined the opening, he realized that the drawers of a small filing cabinet in the boy's room had been pulled open from within and were now blocking ingress into the room. Romeo was in his crib, and even had he not been, he was too small to have pulled the drawers open on his own. Had the ghost-hunting team done this upon leaving the room? How could they? Once the drawers were pulled open, their egress would have been blocked as well.

A confounded Aaron went to the kitchen and grabbed a screwdriver, which he then used to methodically push the drawers closed. Once inside the room, he approached the crib only to find the infant was wrapped up in a blanket. Wrapped very tightly, in fact. Aaron quickly unwrapped the tyke, and then, as he explained, "as soon as I unwrapped the blanket, he just took this big gasp of air and then started breathing normally again."

Try as he might, Aaron could find no logical explanation for the event. How did the drawers get opened from within the room?

How had Romeo gotten wrapped so dangerously in his own blanket? Aaron was shaken by the event, so shaken that he consented to another investigation.

When our team investigated the room, we found that the floorboards by the door had some play in them. It is an older structure and the floors are, not surprisingly, springy. Even so, walking in and out of the room and even jumping up and down in the doorway did not cause the drawers of the filing cabinet to open. We could not get the drawers to roll out on their own. Had the motherly entity Lindsey reported tried to protect Romeo from the strangers she thought were threatening him? If so, she had come dangerously close to smothering the child.

Our First Investigation

When Lindsey first contacted me, I came out and did a walk-through of the home and conducted a fairly lengthy interview with her. I admit I was somewhat skeptical of her claims. As with every case I investigate, I try to go in with an open mind, looking for logical explanations first, before believing that all things are paranormal. While she was adamant about her claims, I thought she might also be prone to belief in the paranormal. Many people develop what I call the "haunted house effect." When they believe a building is haunted, whether it is or not, then everything that isn't immediately explainable is attributed to the ghost. Lose your car keys, the ghost took them. Hear a thump, it must be the ghost. With all the television "reality" shows on the paranormal, belief in or at least awareness of the paranormal has been on the rise, resulting in a type of hyperphasmaphobia.

Full investigations absorb a lot of time, energy, and resources—my resources. I admit I'm often hesitant, sometimes too hesitant, to make the commitment if I feel there will be no payoff in the end.

Lindsey also told me that most of the activity happened between the wee hours of the morning, between two and three a.m. Despite my love of paranormal investigating, I am not what you would call a night owl, and, thus, staying up all night was not all that tempting. My team typically arrives in the early evening before sundown so that we have some natural light during setup. Setup can take one to two hours, depending on the size of the building and the amount of equipment we have to set up. We often only investigate for three hours before breaking down and departing. We're usually heading out of an investigation around eleven. This may not sound like a lengthy amount of time. However, if we run four video cameras, each recording three hours of footage, and a like number of audio recorders, we then have a whopping twenty-four hours of material to review. Thus, even a short investigation requires a herculean effort on the part of the investigators.

But when I first heard about the investigation, I was only too eager to get my hands dirty. On our first investigation, I brought Gene and a new investigator named Shay. We brought minimal equipment, as it was a short investigation. The first time we investigated the home was in the dead of winter, and the family was present, as were the dogs and the cat. The infant was in his crib wide awake and babbling to himself the whole time. I've already mentioned the child's strange nocturnal habits. Having no wish to disturb the child, we were never able to check out the room, but we spent the majority of the evening in the family room while Aaron and Lindsey departed to the master bedroom in order to give us some privacy.

Contamination was obviously a factor. I never like to investigate a building with that much human and animal activity going on. But putting the family out of their house on a cold winter's night just wasn't an option. Still, when analysis of the audio and video was done, I came away with two possible anomalous sounds: one a clear, audible sigh caught in the kitchen, possibly one of the dogs, and the other a male voice answering "What is your name?" with what sounded like "Wade." That and the picture of the unexplained mist in the dining room were enough incentive to do another investigation. What I especially liked about the mist picture was that there was a picture taken beforehand that didn't show a mist and a picture shortly after that that also showed no mist.

The "Wade" EVP was interesting. Rarely do we get an answer when asking the entity's name, which makes our job that much more difficult. Was Wade someone who rented from Goldberg? Then again, the two homes were moved from unknown locations, and we haven't been able to check the deeds of former property owners to confirm a Wade.

However, the voice might also have been saying something else that just sounded like Wade to me. Just once I'd like a voice to answer, "Well, my name is John Parker III, and I died in this house in 1914." Until that fantasy comes true, I have to caution my clients not to read too much into what is said and to spend more time trying to figure out what is happening versus who is doing it.

Our Second Investigation

I was still intrigued enough to return for another investigation. There'd now been two investigations that had both provided some evidence. This time I decided we'd do a lengthier investigation and really try to get to the bottom of the activity. It was late summer and the family was decamping to the family summer cottage. Even the dogs would be absent, and we would have the house all to ourselves. We returned with a four-person team, a wonderful number for a small residence, as two could investigate while the other two manned the surveillance camera system.

It was a dark and stormy night when we returned to the Hartly house. No, really, it was a thunderous night with sheeting rain and lightning. Just the kind of dreamy night of ghost hunting I love. It's not because of the ambience, although investigating in a storm does set a mood. No, it's all that energy that is released into the environment that helps fuel paranormal activity. A thunderstorm releases a plethora of negatively charged ions, little electrically charged particles. These particles get absorbed almost immediately in the environment, but while they're present, they're available as a possible source of energy for a spirit, or so the theory suggests. It's believed that a spirit is willful energy, but like humans, who require food to fuel our bodies, ghosts require energy. They can acquire this energy from man-made sources of electromagnetic energy, hence the often-reported battery drains in video cameras or flashlights. However, they can also acquire it from natural sources, such as the latent energy available in air humidity and the ions that are released during a thunderstorm. This may be the reason why so much more paranormal activity occurs around sources of water.

Other groups have experimented with ion generators, hoping to mimic Mother Nature by creating and releasing ions, but they have not recorded a demonstrable uptick in paranormal activity. Ion generators also lead to an increase in particulate matter—thousands more "orbs" on your infrared (IR) camera to watch. Like everything in the paranormal field, there never seems to be a clear and concise answer.

We were still setting up our equipment when the activity started. In particular, we were placing the voice recorder and setting up a surveillance camera in the vicinity of the hall closet when we noticed the hair on the back of our necks was standing on end. It's one thing to creep yourself out during an investigation and another to have it happen when you're not paying any attention, when you're just going about your business, so to speak. And it happened to me as well as the others. I'm about as sensitive as a stone, and I tend to be skeptical in nature. So it's odd for me to have an attack of the heebie-jeebies, especially of the magnitude I was experiencing—repeatedly.

We had set up our equipment and were preparing to head out the door for a quick dinner when we obtained our first EVP of the night, which we discovered on evidence review. It was a female voice we would hear many times on tape, asking, "Why?" We captured it in the hall closet. I'm guessing she was questioning why we were there. The entire team was in another part of the building at the time.

On the second investigation, I brought two brand-new investigators along, Renne and Maya, and Shay, who had only one investigation under his belt, the previous trip to the Hartly house. The team was running around with their ambient thermometers recording every single degree drop or gain. They were very new at the time and demonstrated the overexuberance typical of beginning investigators. I was new myself once as well, so I understood the desire to find anything at all. Finally, I got a little exasperated and decided to show them what a significant temperature change actually entailed. So we gathered in the family room for a session with my IR thermometer. Unlike ambient thermometers, which read the air temperature in the room, IR thermometers bounce an infrared light beam off solid objects and gauge the temperature of solid objects. That's why I don't typically use them to find cold spots in a room any longer. I have found them interesting to use in temperature experiments, however. I chose a spot on an interior wall, a wall without plumbing. It was summer, and the house did not have central air. The windows were closed due to the rain.

As much as possible, I try to limit the amount of contamination that can come from running heating or cooling systems. Even if it means sitting in a sweltering family room in summer. I sat down on the floor, pulled out my IR thermometer, and announced to the room, "Okay, show me what you've got."

With Shay's gasp of disbelief and the giggles from the women in the room, our recording commenced.

"All right, I'm at 75.5 degrees," I said. I was over by the voice recorder and indicated where the IR beam was recording temperature. "I want you to take it down to 75.0. Can you take it down to 75.0?"

Shay reported on the record that his ambient thermometer, which was sitting on the coffee table in front of the couch, was reading 74.3 degrees.

With the IR thermometer set in a specific location, I asked the spirit to take the temperature down in small, half-degree steps. The overall temperature in the room didn't change—it was just in the area at which my beam was directed. I was looking for a significant decrease of 8 to 10 degrees in the end, not the 1-to-2-degree fluctuation that goes on all the time in a room. But I've found if I do it in half-degree steps, I'm able to control the drop with my voice commands.

I've been very successful with this approach. It appears that, when it works, the spirits can control either the temperature or the meter in very precise ways if they're not asked to do too much too quickly. Notice for example that my gauge was not reading 74.3 (like Shay's) but showed a multiple of 0.5. I've had this experiment work only on a handful of investigations, but when it does work, it is rather remarkable in its accuracy. However, when we placed an ambient temperature gauge in the vicinity of where I was getting the readings, it indicated that the spot was the same temperature as the room, which led me to believe that it might not have been the temperature that was being manipulated but the actual gauge itself. I believe that spirits, being willful energy, find it rather easy, once they get the hang of it, to manipulate electronic equipment.

The group put their meters on the coffee table so that they could monitor the temperature during the experiment. This transcript excerpt, which begins a few minutes into the recording, illustrates the significant drop measured on the temperature gauge, which had started at 75.5 degrees.

ROBIN: Please and thank you. 69.0, please. 69.0. It's 69.0. 68.5, please. 68.0. (*Pause*) 68.0, thank you. 67.5, please. 67.0. 66.5?

MAYA: Please and thank you.

ROBIN: Please and thank you. 67.0. Can you take it to 66-point—ah, there we go. 66.5, 66.5. 66.0? (*Almost immediately*) There we go.

MAYA: Wow, that's amazing. You're amazing.

ROBIN: Ah, 66.0. Don't lose it, don't lose it, don't lose it.

MAYA: Go on, you can do it.

ROBIN: 66.0.[7] There we are, 66.0. For the record. 65.5, please. 65.5, please. 65.5, 65.5.

MAYA: Please and thank you. Beautiful.

---

7. I'm noticing that it's starting to slip as if something is running out of the energy that it takes to maintain the change. I've found usually that 8 to 10 degrees is about as far as the entity can maintain it.

ROBIN: 65.0, please. 65.0, please. [It's] 65.0. 64.5? (*To the group*) Now that's what I'm talking about. 64.0. (*Almost immediately*) There we go. 64.0, 64.0.

MAYA: For the record, what does your temperature gauge say?

RENNE: Ah, mine says 75.7.

ROBIN: 64.0?

MAYA: What does mine say?

RENNE: Yours says 75.3.

MAYA: Shay, what does yours say?

SHAY: 74.3.

MAYA: And what is your infrared saying right this minute?

ROBIN: 64.0. Beautiful. What [temperature] did we start at?

They are now seven minutes into the experiment, and none of them can remember the exact starting point.

MAYA: You have it on video, don't you?

ROBIN: Yeah, I do. 63.0? 63.0? We're stuck at 63.5. Come on, baby. Come on, baby.

MAYA: I'd say 10 or 11 [degrees difference], maybe even 12.

ROBIN: It's a bloody good show, that's what it is.

A few minutes later, the temperature on Robin's gauge has continued to drop, while the temperature on the ambient thermometers has actually risen a couple of degrees.

SHAY: Mine is still at 74.3.

Robin: Shit. (*Maya immediately corrects her.*)

Robin and Maya together: 62.5. Thank you, and I'm sorry if I offended you.

Maya: They're very amused. Renne, what is the temperature on yours?

Renne: It's still 75.7 on mine and 75.1 on Shay's.

Robin: [The owners of the house] told me that this was the room where all the action happened. I guess they weren't kidding.

The starting temperature on my IR gauge was 75.5 degrees Fahrenheit and the ending was 62.5, a total of 12.5 degrees of change. Throughout the experiment, the average temperature in the room didn't change more than a degree or two.

During the course of the evening, we captured numerous EVPs, most of which appeared to be of the same female speaker. I also had a clear exhale captured in an empty room, which gave some credence to the sigh I had captured on the first investigation.

One of the theories about ghosts is that they are a type of imprint of a personality in an environment. It may be as simple as leaving DNA in an area, which we do all the time. Touch a doorframe and you leave a fingerprint of skin cells. Every cell in our bodies contains a complete set of our genetic DNA, a complete blueprint of ourselves. And there is evidence that one of the jobs of DNA is to act as a receiving mechanism for information.

For example, scientists have studied organ recipients who have reported personality changes after receiving an organ. Sometimes it's subtle: for instance, suddenly liking foods they hadn't before. Other times the change is profound, with the recipient adopting the personality of the deceased. DNA is powerful and also not fully understood. Much of the DNA strand, what scientists have so far dubbed "junk DNA," may actually have another purpose, the purpose of receiving outside information. If we accept that consciousness may exist outside the body versus in the brain, then DNA may act as a type of satellite receiver.

When we die, our life force—that low-level energy that animates our bodies, moves our muscles, pushes impulses across our synapses—departs. As we know from science, energy is never created nor destroyed, though it can change form. What if that freed energy now used the DNA in the environment as a type of transmitter?

Thus, this remnant of a person might start acting in ways that are similar to the whole self, as if it were simply a copy. In this way, we can compare a spirit to a digital file. Some files get interrupted during the copying process, and as a result, only some of the file is transferred. Our lowest-level residual haunt would fall into this category. The haunting phenomenon happens when environmental triggers cause the file to play. And like a CD or DVD, when it does play, it always plays the same file. Hence, the phenomenon is always the same, and it does not interact with people or even acknowledge the presence of them. The shadowy figure Lindsey reported seeing is an example of this type of phenomenon, as it always moved from the center of the room toward the window in the same pattern.

The more complete a copy the more interactive the spirit might be and the more intelligent it might seem to appear. Even at their most complex, however, ghosts don't really seem to be living beings. They might be able to answer simple questions. For example, you might ask "Are you happy in this house?" and get a "yes" response, but they don't adapt and change as a human does. They don't appear to have a firm understanding of the passage of time, for example. Whatever seems to reside in the hall closet may be stuck in the closet because it can't fathom that the house is now joined with another building.

It seemed that Lindsey and Aaron's female spirit was a far superior spirit in that she could interact with and sense changes in her environment. A very chilling EVP at the height of the storm demonstrated just such an intelligence. Our one male investigator, Shay, was in the master bedroom with Maya. Through the rushing rain, a female voice caught on a recorder in the hall closet said, "Yes, I see him," as if talking to someone else. The fact that there was only one male in the building that night and that he was at the time in the master bedroom to which the closet opens demonstrates a remarkable awareness on the part of the female spirit. Indeed, it was this EVP as much as anything that happened that night that unnerved Shay. Well, that and a personal experience he had in the master bedroom that he described as being "punched in the stomach by a push of energy." So unnerved was he by the house that he quit the team immediately after the investigation.

After several hours of investigating, we decided to bed down for a few hours of rest, with the idea that we would resume during the two to three a.m. timeframe, when the homeowners insisted they had the most activity. Two of us rolled out sleeping bags in the master bedroom. Shay lay down on the family room couch and immediately fell asleep. Maya, our team night owl, set up her computer and started working on her laptop. At some point late in the night, with everyone else asleep, she reported that suddenly every clock in the house started ticking loudly, preternaturally loudly. And then, without warning, the rocking chair across the room creaked as if someone had just sat down. Maya acknowledged that something had tried to alert her to its presence.

Upon evidence review, we found that throughout the rest of the evening our female resident chimed in on conversations about music and horses, often launching right in over the conversation, although we didn't know it at the time. Renne and I were finishing our last session in the baby's room at around three, and I had just announced we were done and going to be leaving. Right before stopping the recorder that was in the crib, we captured an excited voice saying, "Hey, okay." I think she'd had enough of us for one evening.

Our Third Investigation

Again Aaron and Lindsey had decamped for the weekend to their summer cabin. Again we would have the house to ourselves. By the third investigation, we were ready for the Hartly house. However, the energy on this investigation was not nearly as palpable as it had been on the second. Still, we captured evidence that was solid.

It was a hot September evening in a house with no air conditioning, and Brian, our newest, token male investigator, and I were heading down the hall to do a session in the master bedroom. Both Maya and Renne, rounding out our team, clearly saw a staticky, misty substance seem to follow us down the hall and into the room on the surveillance camera. Subsequent review of the footage, however, proved disheartening. Unfortunately, the quality of the camera footage was not such that we could see anything clearly enough to actually call it evidence.

We had a few instances that evening of what I'll simply dub "evidence layering." Layering is when you seem to have more than one type of evidence going on in one session. For example, Maya and Renne were in the hallway conducting a session and they were talking about music.

"Do you like classical music?" Renne asked.

On an EVP later found by the team, a very distinct female whisper that sounded like "*bar-ee*" was captured. While both clear and distinct, it didn't really appear to make much sense. But then a moment later, Maya reported a personal experience and then an EMF spike.

"I just got a chill up my arm—0.2," Maya said. She referred to the EMF gauge they had with them, indicating a sudden change in the electromagnetic field. "And it's steady."

They paused for a few seconds. "And it's blank," Maya reported. The meter had gone back down to 0.

"We're trying to see if we can play just a little bit of music," Renne offered, "if you want to stay around and listen."

This exchange is exciting because we have a personal experience (the chill up the arm), the measurable EMF change in the environment, and a documented disembodied voice. This type of layering makes me a very happy investigator.

Another such exchange occurred in the storage room when Brian and I conducted a session. I had my dowsing rods out and they appeared to be reacting to my questions. Sometimes I can seemingly employ them as a means of communication. I don't present my "findings" with the dowsing rods as evidence to homeowners. I use them more to get a feeling or impression of an area, although I've been impressed over the years by their seeming accuracy. They don't work that neatly in every location, but in the Hartly house, they always do. In fact, I've had much the same conversation with the same female spirit every time I investigated the house, and the fact that she has always answered my questions in the same way is rather remarkable, if not reassuring.

In the video clip I presented to the homeowners, I again found an interesting layering of activity going on. Below is the transcript.

While it might seem as if I'm peppering the spirit mercilessly with questions, in reality I pause between questions for eight to ten seconds—or more if the rods seem like they're going to answer a question. I reported a barometric pressure of 101.8 in the room and began.

ROBIN: Are you here with us?

The rods turn in a lazy fashion.

ROBIN: Can you speak your name into one of the cameras? Either the one on the desk or the one in Brian's hand? What is it you want us to tell Lindsey and Aaron? Is the woman here? Can the woman come and talk to us? We know you're here... I would love it if you made one of those devices go off (*referring to a dual EMF and temperature gauge*).

ROBIN: I'm feeling you on my leg, I think. (*To Brian*) I'm feeling chills. Are you getting chills?

BRIAN: Huh?

ROBIN: I said, are you getting chills?

BRIAN: Ah, not really.

ROBIN: Okay. I'm getting major chills all along my leg.

Feeling the static electrical sensations, she stops and moves her EMF-temperature gauge closer to her legs to see if it registered anything. It didn't, so she continues.

ROBIN: Are you here with us? Maybe it's just the night air coming in.

She picks up the rods and they resume their gentle spin.

ROBIN: Is the woman here?... Yeah, I thought maybe you were here. I never did get a straight answer. How many children did you have? Do you remember? Are you looking for your children? Do you miss them? Is that why you remain in this house—are you waiting for your children to come? They didn't abandon you, did they? Is that why you like the little boy so much?[8]

The rods continue to do a noncommittal, gentle spin.

ROBIN: Did you maybe lose them—did you lose your children? Maybe you woke up one day and couldn't find them?[9] Are you mad with me? Can you walk up to one of the devices and make them go off? You're starting to get annoyed or upset? About your children? Is it about your children? (*The left rod starts to pick up some speed.*) Did they go away and leave you? Or did you lose them? Do you think maybe you died and that's why you couldn't find them anymore? Had you thought of that? Do you like the family that lives here? Do they remind you of your family?

There's a long pause and the rods slow down, resuming their gentle circles.

ROBIN: Are you trying to tell me something? What is it you want me to know?

The rods continue to slow.

---

8. The woman and I are old acquaintances by now. We've had much the same conversation several times, and she always seems to give me the same vague responses. She was older when she passed away. She'd had children who had grown and left her. Now she was lonely, but she cared for the family in whose home she now resided and especially liked the baby boy.

9. I'm working off an idea that maybe she passed away and didn't realize why she could no longer find her children. If you've ever watched the wonderful movie *The Sixth Sense*, you might understand the premise. I speculate that sometimes people pass quickly or unexpectedly, and their spirit, that imprint that's left behind, has no clear idea what's going on. As Cole Sear, the young character in the movie, says, "They don't know they're dead."

ROBIN: I'm getting a strange sensation on my right shoulder. And I'm getting this strange *krrr krrr* sensation in my right ear. It's an electrical charge. (*The left rod stops entirely and the right swings slowly back and forth to the right.*) It's weird.

Robin stops to shake her right shoulder and shake out the rods.

ROBIN: Are you still there? Are you trying to talk in my ear? Tell me more about the children. How many children did you have?

The left rod stops moving entirely, but the right spins slowly and lazily in full circles.[10]

ROBIN: (*To Brian*) Maybe it was something to do with the rods, but I don't recall ever having that feeling before.

Suddenly, the left rod starts spinning with some vigor.

ROBIN: (*To Brian*) That's not me. We seem to get the most reaction when I'm talking about the children. (*To the spirit*) Tell me more about the children. Were they good children? Did they treat you with respect? Were they bad children? (*The rods spin with more vigor.*) Did they grow up and leave you? Or did they just go and find their own lives? It's painful when that happens, isn't it? Did you have grandchildren?

Brian turns around and looks out the door as Maya's voice is heard. A moment later, Maya appears in the doorway.

MAYA: Hey, we're getting some activity up front.

ROBIN: Okay.

MAYA: We're picking up stuff.

---

10. Note that I'd indicated it was on my right side that I'd had the experience in my ear.

ROBIN: On the monitors?

MAYA: Ah, we saw a couple of things. Something in the middle of the hallway here. And something tickled Renne's ear and pulled her hair.

ROBIN: Huh.

MAYA: And we got a spike of a 2.5 [on the EMF gauge] and things like that.

Maya departs back to the kitchen.

ROBIN: (*Jokingly*) Why don't I ever get a spike? But I was definitely getting that ... strange feeling. Maybe it's the night air. Oh, but the window is not open.

It was at this point I realized that the strange sensation on my leg and ear couldn't have been caused by the night air coming in the window as the window was closed. I isolated this section of the video to show to the client because I thought it was interesting. I experienced some odd sensations that I had at first attributed to a draft. Perhaps when I proved unresponsive to the sensations, the spirit had sought the attention of the other ladies. Remember how at one point my rods had all but stopped moving.

As I isolated the clip on the final DVD I burned for the client, I had a little surprise. When I had asked the entity to go up to one of the cameras and make its presence known, a soft female voice responded, "Okay." I hadn't heard it on the first review. It appeared she had gone out of her way to do just as I had requested.

By the end of the investigation, in the wee hours of the morning, I think we had worn out our welcome with our unseen acquaintance. We were preparing to break down the equipment when we got an EVP, a female voice that commanded us to "get out." Then, about twenty seconds later, she reiterated in an exasperated tone: "Get out. Get out now." Both EVPs were clear and easily understood.

We dragged our weary selves out of there, just as my friend requested, at around five a.m.

The Evidence

This compilation comes from the evidence report of our *second* investigation, the investigation that produced the most evidence. This is just the material that I later presented to Lindsey and Aaron along with time stamps, and I didn't include myriad clips that I threw out as not being strong enough evidence or suspect.

Setup

- Maya's audio recorder was on the crib mattress recording throughout the night.
- Renne's audio recorder was recording in the master closet most of the evening. All EVPs she recorded were from the closet.
- Robin's audio recorder was set up for several hours in the family room but was also used handheld at times.
- Shay's audio recorder was handheld.
- Four stationary cameras were recording all night long, one shooting into the dining room from the family room, two shooting hallways, and one shooting the baby's room.

Baby's Room EVPs

"I don't know." Robin and Maya were doing some EVP work in the master bedroom when this EVP was caught on

Maya's recorder, which was unmanned in the crib. No one was in the baby's room at the time.

"Hey, okay." This was captured on Robin's audio recorder at around three a.m. during Renne and Robin's last session before breaking down. The EVP was captured just as they decided to start breaking down.

Family Room EVPs

Robin and Maya were investigating the other side of the house. Renne and Shay were at the kitchen table monitoring the surveillance cameras. While the two were conversing, there appeared to be a female spirit who desired to get in on the conversation—all three EVPs are during the same hour.

Whispering. There was distinct whispering as Renne talked about getting chills.

"Yes." Shay was talking about wearing some type of protection, such as a cross or rosary, and the voice seemed to agree with him.

Indistinct whispering. Renne talked about her daughter and horses, and the voice was heard again and seemed to be talking about horses as well.

Master Closet

"Why." During setup, crew in the other room talked about ordering dinner. The recording caught a distinct "why" and then "what."

"I can see him." When this was recorded, Renne and Shay were in the master bedroom while Robin and Maya were at command central.

Exhalation in empty room. Renne and Shay were at command central, and Robin and Maya were out on the back deck.

"Goin." Robin and Maya announced they were starting a session, and Renne and Shay were at command central.

"Has it." Robin and Maya were in the baby's room doing the session, and Renne and Shay were at command central.

Final Assessment

The Hartly house landed us a bounty of EVPs over the years. Mostly, the speaker on the recordings was female and sounded like the same female. As I said before, she appeared to have intelligence and left us EVPs on a host of different subjects, from horses to children. She seemed acutely aware of her environment. She even commented on Shay's attendance, saying, "Yes, I see him." I find this EVP fascinating because there was only one male at the investigation or anywhere on the property that night. The EVP was captured in the master bedroom, where Shay was conducting a session at the time. Even odder was the fact that it sounded like the female spirit was speaking to someone else, perhaps the male apparition that is witnessed in this limited area of the building.

The female apparition also appeared to have a will of her own. During the third investigation, Brian asked, "Are you the one who took care of the little boy?" In an EVP she appeared to respond, "Don't ask me that."

She was also capable of mood changes. Earlier in the evening of the second investigation, she appeared to be conversing with Shay and Renne about horses and later with Maya and Renne when they were talking about shopping, in a rather lighthearted way. Later in the wee hours of the morning, she became exasperated with us when we simply wouldn't leave, and commanded us to depart, with two remarkably clear EVPs, one saying, "Get out," and one slightly later saying, "Get out now."

The male spirit was more elusive. We were never able to catch him on film or video, although we did have the picture with the mist that was captured in the dining room. And we've only ever captured two EVPs with a male voice. The first one occurred on the first investigation and seemed to answer "Wade" to my question about his name, as I said before. The second male EVP occurred as we were breaking down our third investigation. Brian had just gone to the back of the house and disconnected a cable running to one of the surveillance cameras. We could hear him on the audio walking back down the hall to the dining room and kitchen. He had just departed the area when the voice was recorded. It was a distinctly male voice and whispered something that was unfortunately indistinguishable.

My final assessment of the Hartly house is that it is indeed haunted. The female spirit appeared to have intelligence. She could detect people in her environment, detect dangers in the house, and interact, at times in a remarkable way, such as the time she shoved Lindsey out of the kitchen. The male spirit may be less intelligent and thus less interactive. He seemed more confused. For one thing, whereas the female spirit appeared to be able to move anywhere in the dwelling, the male spirit seemed rather stuck near the environs of the hallway closet, master bedroom, and small area of hall.

Let me spend a moment talking about the hallway closet with the odd ingress and egress. To be clear, it's the same closet in which Lindsey saw the heat-wave mist and the dark figure staring at her one night. And it's the doorway in which their friend witnessed the figure walking through into the master bedroom. During the second investigation, we would be doing mundane activities in the closet, setting the camera up or checking to see if an audio recorder was still functioning, and experience several sudden, unexplained, staticky electrical sensations—in other words, the rather cliché experience of the hair standing up on the back of your neck for no apparent reason. Voice recorders placed in the closet never failed to record unexplained voices.

For some unknown reason, that same closet seemed to be the focal point of much of the activity that occurred in the house, at least the activity that is of a surlier nature. It begged the question, what's up with that strange closet?

The closet was located at the juncture where the two buildings were joined. One of our investigators and self-proclaimed sensitive, Maya, speculated that the closet located where one building ended and the other began acted as a type of barrier to the male entity. Perhaps because the other structure was not there when the entity resided in the home, it now could not cross the threshold. It's as logical an explanation as we have for why the entity appeared to be almost territorial in his inhabitance of the space.

Postscript

During my four-year working relationship with the family, young Romeo has grown from an infant to a precocious child. (I, oddly, have stayed exactly the same youthful age as I've always been.) While he may have accepted his matronly protector out of hand as an infant, as he's grown older, he's also grown wiser. Almost immediately after our third investigation, he apparently had a ghostly encounter that left him fearful of being alone in his room at night. Recall the incident of the blocked door directly after the first investigation. I theorize that our female entity is extremely protective of Romeo, and for whatever reason fears for his safety from strangers.

I received a disturbing email from Lindsey a couple of months after our third investigation of the house. She said that the activity in the boy's room had taken a turn for the worse. He had awoken one night screaming that he had seen a ghost and demanding to be let out of the room. For long nights afterward, he insisted on sleeping with them in the master bedroom and refused to enter his own room even during the day. What was she to do? I suggested she try to speak with the boy calmly so as not to scare the absolute bejesus out of the tyke, and she should try to talk about his experience without influencing him in any way. What she did next I thought was brilliant: she made it into a game.

Using a pool soaker—the kind that has a noodle body and sucks up the water only to shoot it out in a long stream—she told her son that they were going to play ghostbusters. Walking through the house, he was to tell her where he had seen ghosts and she would suck them up. He dutifully showed her where he had seen entities, and she sucked them up. Incidentally, the boy indicated the same spots that we had determined to be active in our investigations. And yes, he most decidedly indicated the hall closet.

This activity did a number of things worth noting. First, it pointed out to a concerned mother where her son was seeing apparitions. The fact that they appeared to correspond with her experiences and with investigation results is validating. Second, she took her son seriously, neither encouraging him to make things up nor discouraging him from communicating with her. But third, and I think this is the most important, it gave mother and son power back. I'm sure they both felt like they were much more in control after the activity.

Additionally, Lindsey's exercise was a good way to communicate with the spirit. I have always felt that if a spirit is in some way an essence of a deceased human, then they are bound by the same upbringing and courtesies with which they were raised. In other words, you can communicate and attempt to set parameters with an unseen houseguest. I think Lindsey's game also went a long way toward doing that, indicating to the spirits that they had been seen, that they had overstepped their boundaries by frightening the boy, and that such behaviors were not acceptable.

It wasn't immediate, but Lindsey eventually got the little tyke sleeping in his own room again and, as far as I know, peacefully. Last time I communicated with Lindsey, she also reported that the paranormal activity had greatly decreased as well.

CHAPTER 3
A DANGEROUS SOUL

Long Neck, Delaware

Probably the all-time most bizarre case I've ever worked on was the Long Neck house investigation. It started with an impassioned voice mail, and then another immediately after, by a man named Scott. Scott was upset. Scott was panicked. Scott was . . . freaked out. And he wanted to talk to me. He wanted to talk to me right now.

I had just finished a long day at work and was heading home to make dinner for my family. However, I took a deep breath, took out an investigation request form and dialed the number.

I got Scott immediately, and he was very happy to hear from me. I usually like to control interviews, take my time, get the details, and try to get to the bottom of what was going on. But that simply wasn't going to happen this time. When people hit a certain level of frightened, it's just fight or flight. And Scott was at that point.

The Backstory

What I got from Scott was that he was working on his girlfriend's house. He was an electrical contractor by trade and in his spare time was helping Louise with a major renovation of a home she had purchased right next to Scott's father's house. She had purchased the home via an estate sale in 2015. Since the home was run-down and in need of major upgrades and repairs, she hadn't actually moved in until April 2016. When the renovations began, much of the activity also began.

The house itself had been built in 1972 by the previous owner, Wilhelm, who had passed away a year and a half ago, in the very house that he'd built. Wilhelm had been the first to buy in the neighborhood. Apparently, being a man who had prized his privacy, he'd purchased the lot the house sat on and the adjoining lot, which Scott's father later purchased before building his own home. Wilhelm lived in the house with a woman listed as his wife, Mary, for many years, and Mary died two years before Wilhelm passed. According to the neighbors, the very day Mary died in the hospital, Wilhelm came home and threw her adult son out of the house. Apparently, the young man had not been his son, though the couple were listed as being married for twenty-some years, and the son in question was eighteen at the time. There are times that legal records leave something to be desired. Reading between the lines, I guessed that this wasn't a home of domestic bliss.

Wilhelm continued living in the residence by himself for the next two years. In poor health, he was wheelchair-bound and spent most of his days and nights in an old recliner. A female neighbor would often look in on Wilhelm. He didn't appear to have any other caregivers.

Having no family of his own, or family that he would claim, when Wilhelm passed away, the house and the adjoining lot next door became the property of an acquaintance, Jeanette, in accordance with his will. Louise recalled that Jeanette was every bit as rough as the late Wilhelm in reputation. The mysterious Jeanette never took up residence in the home and failed to pay the property taxes. Thus, the home stood vacant and eventually fell into foreclosure, at which time Louise was able to purchase it, along with what was left of Wilhelm's personal possessions. Louise had shrewdly purchased the run-down home in the resort community, probably realizing that it was an excellent investment. She had left Wilhelm's furniture in place during the renovation, not wishing to soil her own, with the intention of dropping it all in the dumpster once the sawdust stopped flying.

Scott's father had similarly purchased the lot next door and built his own home when the adjoining property went up for foreclosure. Thus, neither Scott nor Louise had ever known the late Wilhelm except by reputation, the subsequent facts being filled in by neighbors who had also lived for years in the development.

Louise closed on the home in October 2015 and started overhauling it immediately. She met Scott when she began working on the property. Again, the paranormal rarely meets our expectations of what a haunted house should look like. There were footers poured already for expansion of the building, though at the time of the investigation the couple was at work on the original structure. Louise told me later that the paranormal activity began with the renovations, and it was the most active when work on the house was in full swing. Sometimes work would cease and then the activity would quieten. The couple assumed that it was the late Wilhelm who was responsible for the odd happenings, as he had been the only owner of the home, and a very private, if not particularly unlikeable individual.

But whatever or whoever was responsible, it was beyond a doubt that something weird was going on in the house. Things were being moved. There were signs showing up in the drywall dust that he couldn't account for. There were also a lot of electronic disturbances. In a later conversation, Scott and Louise explained to me in more detail about the odd electronic malfunctions. Louise recalled a strange occurrence with the doorbell. She'd purchased a doorbell with a remote sensor, but she'd never actually mounted the doorbell by the front door. She had plugged in the unit that hung on the interior wall, however. The doorbell was in the cabinet in its box, awaiting mounting. One day Louise distinctly heard the doorbell. She thought it was on TV, but she looked at the screen and noticed that it was playing a courtroom drama. Another day Louise contended that Scott was gone and she again heard the doorbell ring three times. That was enough for her. She unplugged the unit from the wall.

One day Scott and his mom were in the house. He recalled coming out of the bathroom and found that the TV was on. He asked his mother if she had turned it on. She said no; she thought he had turned it on. Neither could explain how the TV had turned on by itself.

The new lights throughout the house were operable by remotes. The remote for the dining room light was always kept on the shelf in the kitchen. Scott recalled he would try the remote several times and the lights wouldn't come on. He explained, "One time I came under the lights to check and see if they were working, and they just came on." The remote had been sitting on the kitchen counter at the time. Other times he would approach the lights because all the tools were in a cabinet along the far wall of the dining room. He'd step under the lights and they would go off. That happened six or seven times. "Finally, I said, 'Screw it, I don't need the lights to go get the tools,' and I stepped over here and the lights would turn on. That happened quite a few times." Lighting anomalies in the dining room happened to Louise as well.

Apparently, lights and doorbells weren't the only electronic devices toyed with. Phone anomalies were also at play, in what appeared to be a diabolical plan to cause discord between the couple. Scott recalled that he would call Louise when she had been away visiting her daughter in California. When they were talking late at night, Scott would only be able to hear every third word she was saying, and then static would fill the line. At the same time, Louise would hear every word clearly. While this might be a simple matter of a poor connection on Scott's end, what was odder was the fact that Louise would be alone in her bedroom at her daughter's house late at night talking to Scott, and Scott would hear other voices on the line. Louise said her daughter and her daughter's husband were asleep upstairs during these episodes.

Scott would say, "Who is there with you?"

"No one," Louise would reply.

"Well, I hear someone talking."

"They're upstairs ... in bed."

Scott later confirmed the odd conversations. "I heard distinct words, talking, like, 'shhh,' 'shut up.' Stuff like that."

"He swore I was talking to someone, and there was no one there," Louise added.

Odd markings in the drywall dust were a constant—fingerprints, messages, words in some case. Scott couldn't fathom how they got there, as it was just the two of them working on the house together.

They both admitted to seeing a dark shadow in one of the back rooms when they were sitting in the bedroom across from the bathroom, as well as a similar dark figure in the family room by the hallway entrance.

Louise had at times acted strangely. And Scott admitted that he had at times acted even more strangely, acted in a way that was completely out of character with his gentler nature. Normal exchanges between the couple had escalated, sometimes for no reason whatsoever, to near violence. He'd never been a violent man, not a man prone to bouts of rage. But since he'd begun working on the property, he'd experienced odd personality changes for which he could not account. He'd flown into rages at the least provocation. Sometimes he couldn't remember periods of time, and then he'd come to and find himself in the act of something inexplicable. They'd had a fight apparently, just a day or so before his impassioned voice mail. The argument began in the house, and Louise admitted it escalated quickly. Fearing Scott might become violent, Louise had tried to leave, heading to the door and getting into her car. Scott admitted that it was at this point that he lost himself, and when he came to, he was jumping up and down on the hood of Louise's car. He had been screaming at her, demanding her not to leave. He had no recollection of how he got there or why he had been so dangerously angry. Not surprisingly, when he did hop down from her car, Louise left in somewhat of a hurry. He implored me to come immediately.

Later I would ask Louise for verification of the fight. Louise recalled the battle, which ended with Scott on her hood. "I remember thinking, *I don't know this person.* I went to the car to get away from him because he was getting angry. It didn't matter—it wasn't about anything in particular. He was just angry, so no matter what I said, it was just wrong. It was nasty, and he was scary. Scary, you know—he would puff his chest out. So I wanted to get away. Just run. I ran to the car, but he caught up. And he hopped on the hood and held on. I remember thinking, *I don't want to hurt this guy, but I also don't want to be anywhere near him.* He never did anything like that before. I said to him in the middle of another terrible argument, 'Who are you?' I looked in his eyes, and it was such hate and vengeance. That's not the way he typically looked at me. That's why I think he was possessed."

I asked, "So he would be acting normally and then he'd just flip?"

"Yeah, and it wouldn't take much."

"And would you remember these episodes?" I asked Scott.

"Yeah, afterward. I was like, what in the hell was I doing on your hood? What was I going to get out of that?"

This hadn't been Scott's first brush with the paranormal. He'd lived in a house in Pennsylvania where he'd experienced paranormal activity. He admitted that in his previous house he would "see things all night, back and forth, back and forth. And my one daughter sees things. She saw a black shadowy thing." He hadn't experienced the strange personality shifts before, but he would sometimes "remember things I didn't know." But this situation was far more serious, far more sinister than simply seeing a shadow figure flitting about a room.

Apparently, the ghost of Wilhelm wasn't the only ghost that Scott was concerned about. He had also witnessed innumerable times the full-bodied apparition of a woman. During the course of an evening when taking a break from renovations, Scott would relax for a few minutes in the recliner. From his position in the chair, he reported that she always seemed to come out of the back bedroom to the left, cross the hall, and enter the back bedroom on the right. Scott would see her almost nightly, sometimes several times in a night. She appeared in period clothing with skirts, a high, buttoned collar, and hair bound up in a bun. He always saw her in the hallway moving in the same direction. According to Scott, from his position in Wilhelm's old recliner, he could see a portion of the hallway to the rear of the house. She was oddly out of place, dressed in Victorian-style garb, in a house built in the '70s. An older woman, Scott confided, she had oddly high cheekbones and a look of seriousness on her face.

Finally, Scott said he felt there was a third spirit, that of a small female child. Some of the drawings in the dust were childish in nature. Rudimentary letters and words appeared, like a child practicing her handwriting. Other times they found what appeared to be pictures. One time it looked like a crude alligator had been drawn on the television, and the couple couldn't account for it. Sometimes it was just swirls and curlicues or small fingerprints. These things appeared to be benign in nature, though bizarre.

I knew that starting the investigation wasn't going to happen immediately, as it was the middle of a work week for me, but I did assure him I'd be down in a couple of days to take a look around.

In the meantime, I suggested he stay out of the house and certainly not sleep there. I also suggested he buy and wear some type of protective necklace or other jewelry depending on what faith he followed, such as a Christian cross or the Jewish Star of David. I picked up the phone immediately after and contacted my dependable comrade in arms, Renne, to see if she would be available. I was concerned about walking into this alone.

The Initial Walk-Through

Renne and I arrived on a sultry June afternoon with humidity thick and heavy, as summer days can be in Delaware. We'd no sooner got out of the vehicle when Scott came running over from next door. The heat wasn't slowing him down: he was as animated as he'd been on the phone. He asked me to dial his girlfriend's phone number, noting that she had been awaiting my call. I got Louise on the line immediately. A levelheaded woman, Louise just wanted to speak with me and assure me that I and the team had her blessing to examine the home, even though she was out of town. I assured her I would call her later after my walk-through and speak with her further about her experiences and what we had found on the walk-through.

It was a typical '70s ranch-style home, devoid of any charm or architectural detail whatsoever. Three bedrooms were off the one central hallway leading from the family room. One centrally located bathroom served the entire house. The couple had nearly gutted it, and it felt somewhat like a war zone, as intense renovations can. Louise owned another home in the area and often stayed there when not working on the remodel. Scott lived next door with his father, a man with whom he was very close. Louise was a levelheaded person, as I said earlier, so the first room she'd gutted and remodeled was the bathroom. Fully refurbished and functional, it was the only room in the house that felt ordered at the time.

During the renovation, Scott and Louise had often lived rough, working on the house until exhaustion struck and then bedding down for the night on the dusty, old furniture that remained. Then they'd get up and do it all over again. If you've ever lived through a renovation, you know that it can get really messy really fast. And to do a total overhaul on an entire house while living in it meant the couple lived in the midst of a disaster zone. Drywall dust covered everything, a stack of wood resided in the family room behind the couch, a large table saw sat square in the middle of one of the back bedrooms. The new flooring had not yet been installed, so we walked on raw wood, dodging the rolls of ancient carpeting that awaited hauling out to the garbage. The bathroom had already been overhauled, with all new cabinets and fixtures, but the other rooms were still covered in dust and tarps.

Scott led us in the front door into the family room, where we assembled around a large coffee table. Almost immediately after we walked in, Scott reacted violently. The coffee table was completely covered with a layer of dust, and it looked like someone had taken two small fingers and dragged them across the tabletop.

"That wasn't there before," Scott exclaimed. "I was in the house earlier, and I swear that wasn't there. See, this is what I told you about. Stuff just shows up in the dust, like fingerprints or pictures." The fingerprints and doodles had started first. Then one day Scott said he'd started finding handprints imbedded on the dusty red couches in the family room. According to Scott, "They were huge handprints, an inch and a half bigger than mine. I called my dad and said, 'Come over here. You've got see this.' I asked the neighbor about Wilhelm, and she said that he was a very big man. And I started seeing these handprints that were an inch and a half bigger than mine, like someone had punched the couch with force."

Scott continued, "And it wasn't just one handprint. I started bringing my dad over. There were two handprints on the couch, and one had a star and the other looked like just a circle was written in the palm, or it was jagged. I took pictures of the handprint on the couch. And my dad tried to recreate them. We pushed in with all of our might, and we got only half as much as that. So we'd brush them off, clear them off, and we'd go away for ten minutes, and they would be there." One time he recalled that the hand appeared reversed. "You know how you push yourself up out of a couch? Well, it wasn't the right hand on the right couch arm, it was the left hand, so it would have been really awkward." It was this handprint in which a star was imprinted. Scott had taken photos of it on his cell phone. However, he couldn't show them to me because the photos had inexplicably disappeared.

During the initial interview, I had pulled out my small handheld video camera so that I could record the event. Oddly, the machine repeatedly malfunctioned. I would hit record and then commence speaking with Scott, only to look down a couple of minutes later to find that the machine had turned off. This happened several times that day, and in total I only came away with a few minutes of video. After the video recorder shut down a few times, I shot Renne an inquisitive look, which Scott detected. He exclaimed, "See, that kind of stuff happens all the time around here." Unaccountable computer malfunctions, phone malfunctions, and lighting fixtures not working properly appeared to be regular occurrences.

I admit that I wasn't overly impressed with the two finger marks on the table. I doubted that his memory was that good. How often have we touched items in our living space without even realizing it? However, I let it go, asking him to show us the rest of the building. He took us down the hall to the bedrooms. The bedroom across the hall from the bathroom was where the couple often slept. One old, tattered recliner and a loveseat were in the room, along with an ancient boom box and a dusty TV. Scott noted that marks had shown up on the dusty screen of the TV as well. Then he pointed at the old recliner. This particular recliner had belonged to Wilhelm. It looked ready for the city dump: the arms were frayed, the seat was worn, and all over there were cigarette burns.

When Scott stayed the night, this is the chair he used. He said the weirdest thing happened to him when he sat down in the chair. Almost immediately, he would feel drowsy and drop off to sleep, inevitably dropping the cigarette he'd been smoking, which accounted for the burn marks. He couldn't explain why he immediately fell asleep in the chair, but it was becoming downright dangerous. On this point I had to agree with Scott wholeheartedly.

And then, he began to explain to us how he felt he was becoming the victim of other odd personality disturbances, as he had alluded to before. He had the blackout while Louise was leaving the other day, which he'd told me about over the phone. He'd actually done this twice, he confessed. And there had been another instance while standing on the front porch with Louise. They were having a routine conversation when suddenly something she said had sent him into a rage. He could not explain why he'd been so enraged, as the discussion had been innocuous up to that point.

Scott had also had a fight with his father, a man with whom he had a wonderful relationship. Right on the porch, he'd been so driven to rage that he'd actually punched his father, throwing the poor man off. Scott said that nothing like that had ever happened to them in the past. The female neighbor who had looked in on Wilhelm in his last few years happened to be walking by this particular evening and witnessed Scott's tussle with his father. Later she would confide to Scott that he'd sounded exactly like the late Wilhelm during the incident; she had said as much to her husband that very evening. The two events were eerily similar, she concluded.

I later interviewed the couple and asked them about the incident with his father. Louise admitted that the fight with Scott's father was starkly out of character.

Louise said, "Scott is really close to his dad. For him to have punched him out like that... That's not like him."

Scott agreed, "I've never punched my dad out in my life."

"And this went on for a number of months. Scott was just not himself."

"It made me think that I was being screwed with. That she was cheating on me or that my dad was lying to me."

"He accused me of sleeping with his father. Like we were making love on the front yard or the back yard. It was the furthest thing from the truth."

"Something was playing with my mind."

Wilhelm was a man with a dark history, a man who may have committed sins that surpassed simple domestic disputes, or so another neighbor informed Scott. The team's inquiries into Wilhelm's past were inconclusive. The records indicated that he'd lived his entire life in the town and worked some type of blue collar tradesman job. His obituary said volumes in what it didn't say. It may have been the shortest obituary ever written. It listed the day of his birth, the date of his passing, and that he'd lived in the town of his birth his entire life. Apparently, Wilhelm hadn't been beloved by many.

Scott couldn't account for his uncontrollable fury. He was scared about what he might do. And he was even more afraid that he might be possessed by the former owner, Wilhelm, to whom they owed that lovely piece of late twentieth-century furniture. Could the rages and the sudden bouts of narcolepsy be something dark left over from the former owner? According to the female neighbor that sometimes took care of Wilhelm, she would at times find him in a diabetic coma, sitting in the very same recliner.

Scott also admitted that his eyesight was declining, everything getting dim. Apparently, Wilhelm had been legally blind. And then Scott reported that his joints started aching, especially his hip and knee joints. The same malady was reported by Wilhelm, who had been wheelchair-bound in his last years. It was only when he stayed a long time in the house that Scott had these experiences; when he was away from the house, he felt just fine.

He then took Renne and me to the back bedroom, where he reported feeling uneasy by the closet. Scott told us about what he felt to be a small female spirit, which was active all through the house but most active in this room.

It was in this bedroom too where he had found Louise one day kneeling on the floor. Louise, who was every bit as active in the renovations as Scott, had actually had one leg amputated below the knee earlier in her life. With a prosthetic she walked normally, but she did find getting up and down on her knees difficult. However, there was Louise, kneeling on the floor and humming to herself, and spread around her were pictures on cheap beige craft paper painted with a child's watercolor set. The paintings looked like those of a small child. On one was a crude rainbow, and on another some rudimentary words had been painted. The art supplies were purchased for a granddaughter who sometimes visited, only Louise's granddaughter hadn't been to visit for quite some time, as she lived in California. So who had painted the pictures, he wondered? Scott asked Louise what she was doing, but according to Scott, she seemed out of it and couldn't account for how she had gotten down on the floor or where the paintings had come from.

He got her up and out of the room, and then he went back in to feel the paint brushes that were in a jar. They were wet. It proved to Scott that Louise had been the painter. When I asked Louise later at the investigation if she had in fact painted the pictures, she admitted she had no recollection of doing so. Scott showed us the pictures, which were remarkably odd, and I took video of the event.

We then proceeded up to the attic, which was sweltering. Here also Louise acted oddly, according to Scott. They had been working up in the attic, but at times she would be up there for hours, humming to herself.

Scott concluded that all of it—from the strange rages to the whispered telephone messages to the huge handprints in the drywall dust—seemed to be part of a master plan, a plan devised by the late Wilhelm. "He was trying to make Louise and me fight. Because when we did, the work on the house would stop for a month. No construction for a month because we would break up. I'd go over to my dad's, and work would stop. That's what he wanted." Louise later agreed with that summation. She admitted that when the work stopped on the house, the activity would also quieten, becoming far less sinister.

Renovations are often cited as the impetus for paranormal activity. In this case, work would progress on the house, the activity would increase, the couple would start fighting, and then they'd break up. Scott would be away, and the activity would cease. The male entity appeared to target Scott for the brunt of his abuse, perhaps because Scott was more sensitive than Louise, by Scott's very admission.

Scott led us back out to the hall where he repeatedly saw the apparition of the woman in period garb. He described the situation further for us when I pressed him for details. Scott admitted he knew she was an apparition. "I could see through her. She wasn't solid. I definitely could see through her." He never pursued her, though he was curious about where she had been going. He said it happened too quickly and that she moved with determination. "She wasn't standing there looking at me. She looked like she was going somewhere," Scott explained.

When I inquired, Scott admitted that the spirit didn't appear to be walking, that her head didn't move up and down as someone who was walking would. Instead, she seemed to be floating past, in a movement that Scott described as more like someone riding a moving sidewalk.

She never acknowledged Scott or seemed to interact with him. She would simply appear to come out of the room, cross the hall (which is when Scott would see her through the two-foot opening of his own door), and cross into the other room. "It almost seemed like she didn't know I was there."

Without a doubt, Scott's first priority, however, was the aggressive male spirit he believed was Wilhelm. The changes in his personality that seemed to clearly parallel Wilhelm's, the uncharacteristic bouts of rage, the periods of time when he seemed to lose himself—all of these had Scott unnerved. Although the couple never saw Wilhelm's physical likeness in clear detail, Scott said that sometimes he'd witness a hulking dark figure in the family room late at night near the hallway entrance. Other times he had witnessed the dark shadowy shape in the back bedroom, the very bedroom where he also witnessed the female apparition. He felt the apparition was male by the very size of the thing. But it had dark, indistinguishable features. It appeared more a lurking shadow.

The female apparition, on the other hand, he witnessed in stark clarity. She wasn't as threatening, as she never appeared to interact with Scott or even acknowledge his presence. However, Scott said Louise would sometimes act very strangely. "I would say, 'Dad, look at her, she's not acting right.'" They'd be working on the house when Louise would start to speak out of character. According to Scott, the soft-spoken Louise would start to act more assertive. "Louise isn't a smart-ass, but suddenly she'd start speaking like that. She was acting very blunt, which is not her normal reaction to things. And I'd look and her cheekbones would be higher. And I'd try to get her to look at her eyes in the mirror, but she wouldn't look. Her pupils would grow and shrink, grow and shrink. That was the only time they would do that."

At this point of the tour, Scott left us to get a feel for the place on our own. We spent some time in the attic but didn't really get much of an impression, and it was just simply too hot to stay up there for any length of time. Renne and I wandered around the rest of the building, including the attic, three bedrooms, kitchen, and family room. We didn't really get much in the way of impressions, and we took base EMF readings, not finding anything anomalous. No one else was in the house. We honestly debated taking the case, as we got minimal impressions from the property beyond Scott's rather wild assertions.

Scott returned and we convened in the family room around the coffee table to discuss timeframes and other details. That's when all three of us noticed that while we'd been in the building, several other markings had appeared in the drywall dust on the table. These looked like scratch marks and little curlicues. One near the edge looked as if it might have been two fingers drawn across the table. It being summer, of course we couldn't rule out bugs, but we didn't see any insects on the table. Likewise, as we were standing there discussing the case, we'd sometimes look back down at the table to find even more marks. I must admit that I had been very skeptical of much that Scott had been telling me, but I couldn't deny that the marks were there, that they were multiplying, and that none of us had noticed them before. What was going on? Renne started snapping photos. Then we set up a time to come back, packed up our equipment, and got ready to leave.

We were outside by the car when I made a hesitant suggestion to Scott. It wasn't Scott's property but Louise's, after all. Therefore, anything in the house belonged to her. But I had an uneasy feeling in particular about the recliner. It is believed that objects, just like buildings, can retain something of their former owners. Often these objects are something with sentimental value, such as a portrait of the person or a religious medal. Then other times the objects themselves can be quite mundane, like the bed someone slept in ... or the recliner in which someone had passed their last grisly days.

"Would it be possible to get rid of the recliner?" I asked.

Scott, who was only too happy to make the strange phenomena stop, asked immediately, "What, like burn it?"

Now I was truly fumbling. Louise was going to return home to not only find furniture gone but also discover it had been burnt to a crisp on her front lawn.

"No, no, I don't mean burn it—just park it on the corner and let the trash collectors take it permanently to its new home."

"But what happens if someone stops and picks it up and takes it home?"

"Well, I suppose they'll get more than just a free chair if that happened," I said, dreading the thought of someone else stumbling upon that sinister item but still not wanting to advocate the destruction of Louise's property. True, the recliner, as I said before, was hardly a figure of majestic stature, but still it belonged to neither Scott nor me. The suggestion of getting rid of the chair around which so many frightening events had occurred struck a chord with Scott.

As Renne and I approached my car in preparation to leave, Scott was already running for the house. And as we pulled out of the driveway and drove off Renne and I could see Scott jackrabbitting across the yard with the recliner, heading toward the firepit. We didn't hang around to witness the event, but, as you probably already guessed—yep, he burned it. He doused that thing down with lighter fluid and burned that chair in a big ole bonfire. I figured I'd have some 'splainin' to do when I talked with Louise that evening.

As it turned out, Louise was only too pleased to have that ratty chair out of her house permanently. If Scott was the figure of panic,

Louise was the voice of reason. Yes, there'd been the fight in which Scott had jumped on her car. Yes, there had been the pictures Scott had found for which she had not an explanation or recollection of having painted. Yes, Scott had gone into rages of late with very little provocation. Yes, she noticed markings in the paint and the dust that she could not explain. Yes, she'd occasionally seen a dark figure in the family room, but just out of the corner of her eye—never full on. She hadn't, however, witnessed the female apparition that Scott reported seeing almost nightly. She believed that there were odd things happening in her house that she could not explain, but she felt that as long as they kept their distance, she was okay with them being there.

She went on to explain her odd mood changes. Spending so much time in the house, with so much energy spent, was taking a toll. One night in particular she recalled chugging an entire pitcher of Kool-Aid in order to gain some energy.

Scott had said that she had been on her feet rocking back and forth, back and forth, back and forth, like a child. Louise admitted she'd done that because she'd been on a sugar high.

This very plausible explanation made many of Scott's claims questionable. Like so much in this case, separating the fact from the fantastical was a challenge. If Louise had been up working for a long period of time in the sweltering attic, she may have been suffering from heat exhaustion. And those claims of the drawings in the drywall dust seemed remarkably easy to ignore until we saw them for ourselves.

The very next day, my email exploded. Scott had burned the chair and couldn't believe what he'd seen. He'd whipped out his phone and took video of the burning but couldn't get the file to upload. He insisted I needed to see the video immediately. He said that he and his father had been standing at the firepit watching the chair burn when they both saw the figure of a man and a girl in the flames. Was it Wilhelm and someone he may have harmed? Then the chair split in half and the flames divided and arced up in devil's horns. I did eventually get hold of the video footage. A careful frame-by-frame analysis showed no man or child in the flames that I could see. I did see the devil's horns that Scott had reported, but I believe there was a perfectly natural explanation for the effect. When the chair split in two, the fire also split in two. The rush of oxygen down the middle caused the flames to spike up suddenly and, voilà, devil horns.

Between the time of our initial walk-through and the team actually getting back out to the site for the investigation, Scott contacted the pastor of a local church and had him come out to the house to perform a house blessing. Whether it was the cross that Scott had begun to wear religiously, the chair being burned, the house being blessed, or the combination of all three, Scott reported that the most sinister of the activity—namely, Scott's taking on the personality of a dead man—had stopped. When we returned, Scott was much calmer.

He also wanted to explain that the electrical devices continued to malfunction in the building. And then his cell phone inexplicably disappeared. It was remarkable, he said, as he never went anywhere without it. He had been forced to purchase a new one. Then he started getting odd calls. An unfamiliar number would appear on the screen. He'd answer the call, and there would be no one there. He wouldn't get a dial tone or a recording or a voice; it would just be dead air. He would hang up and attempt to call the number back, but he always got a recording saying that the number was not in service. If he tried the number on the landline, the number would ring through to a clicking sound. Apparently, all he would get was a strange clicking sound that would continue for as long as he stayed on the line.

Again I was skeptical. Telemarketers came to mind. But I decided to call the number and see for myself. What happened next was *truly* odd, even for someone who works with the odd all the time. I dialed the number on Louise's landline, and while I was waiting to see if the call went through, my investigator Brian's cell phone rang. It was an unknown number. He answered the phone and got dead air. I got a recording saying the number was not in service. Brian and I merely stared at one another completely perplexed. *What in the world*, I thought, *just happened?*

I had long been open to the idea that the dead can make contact with the living using an electronic device, such as a telephone. I'd just never experienced it firsthand, nor had I met anyone who had. Still, I wasn't convinced and decided to do a little more research before claiming it was paranormal. As I said, telemarketers came to mind, as they often try to mask their true identity. Oddly, when I did an online search into whether a phone number can function (call) in one direction only, one of the first articles to pop up was about this phenomenon being paranormal. Scott's experiences actually met the criteria for the most often reported scenario: mainly, a spirit tapping into the low level of energy in a phone line or cell phone and manipulating the device to make it ring. In the majority of the cases, one would answer it and just simply get dead air. The premise of the article was that while a spirit didn't find it all that difficult to make a phone ring, they did find it difficult to actually speak through it.

The Investigation

Maya, Brian, and I began the setup process as Louise and Scott departed to do some shopping. We set up the camera surveillance system to record footage in the back bedroom where the couple had reported seeing the shadowy figure. One covered the family room/living room area, in particular the coffee table where we had witnessed the weird scratch marks. With permission from Louise, we very carefully washed and dried the coffee table. Then we covered the table completely in flour in as uniform a covering as we could manage. We trained a camera on the table and couches so that we could see any changes in the flour as they occurred. We placed another camera in the back bedroom where Louise had apparently completed her painting masterpieces. We set up audio recorders in various locations and then went to work.

Being such a small team, we separated, Brian staying back to watch the surveillance camera feed located in the kitchen while Maya and I did a thorough sweep of the house. Then we swapped and Maya watched the feeds as Brian and I investigated. Probably the most remarkable occurrence we witnessed that night was when we stepped outside to take a break. Maya's EMF detector spiked outside around the footers poured for the new addition. She took off on a crusade with EMF detector in hand, reporting that she had detected EMF anomalies within a hundred-foot radius around the building. The fields seemed to fluctuate as well, meaning that the detector would spike and then plunge back to zero as if something was moving about.

We conducted sessions in all the various rooms over the course of the next couple of hours, but our meters detected very little, as did we ourselves. Then Maya suggested we call Louise and Scott back to the location. Perhaps they had spent so much time in the building and connected with the entities to the point that nothing would occur without them also in the building.

Nearly on cue, the couple arrived at the house, wondering how the investigation was going. We invited them in and asked them to participate in a session with us.

I had wanted first to present a plausible explanation for the shadowy figure Scott had witnessed in the back-right bedroom. We had noticed during the investigation that when someone stood in the hallway by the door, backlit by the hallway light, they would cast a very strong shadow on the back wall of the bedroom/workshop. I had thought we might have debunked the shadow man, but Scott proved me wrong. He and Louise had witnessed the shadow along the interior wall by the breaker box, not the back wall where our shadows had cast.

We began the session now with Scott and Louise in attendance, and Scott started by confirming that Wilhelm had died in the house, in the family room where the red carpet rolls were awaiting their fate: "The room with the red carpet—that's where he died."

Scott implored the spirits, "Just like the last time I told you, bud. Now is the time to show yourself."

Immediately, Maya reported an EMF spike of 9.4 as she stood in the hallway near the entrance to the family room. It was the same area where Scott reported seeing the black figure.

Scott also tried to talk to the child spirit who had "left her initials on one of the drawings."

About this time, with all of us in the side room bedroom across from the bathroom, Maya reported a 2.0 spike on her EMF meter, again in the hallway, followed by a 0.9 and then a 0.4. Before Louise and Scott returned, we hadn't been getting any EMF spikes, so the night seemed to have gotten somewhat more interesting.

Then Maya reported feeling chills in the hallway. "We're not here to hurt you; we're here to help you communicate. I implore something to put a fingerprint in the flour," she called out. "Steadiest reading I've had—0.3."

Maya asked Louise and Scott, "What was the timeline for when you started noticing things?"

"It happened just as soon as I walked in. I started seeing shadows at the left side of the cabinet peeking in at me," answered Scott, referring to the family room. "As I said before, Louise had left Wilhelm's existing furniture in place until the renovations of the house were complete."

He continued, "We would be on the couches sleeping. All night she sat there, and I was there, and I started seeing shadows peeking in all night. I would see shadows peeking around the [TV] cabinet. And we had drywall stacked there, and I would see shoulders and a head peeking out at me all night. She would see me looking at it, and I would act like it wasn't there."

Scott then referred to episodes he'd had in the recliner. "I would be sweating, sitting on that chair, and then I'd be freezing." These odd shifts in body temperature might be attributable to someone suffering from an illness or disease. "And my vision started going bad in the last eight weeks. The neighbor said Wilhelm had been nearly blind. And I was like, 'Oh my God.' Did I tell you about the two and a half hours I'd pass out? They said he would sit in that chair in a diabetic coma for hours. I started doing it. I'd be in that chair passed out for two and a half hours."

Scott admitted that all the happenings had "cost me huge, huge," referring to the emotional and physiological output associated with channeling the spirit whether wittingly or unwittingly.

Maya cut in, "Robin, I just felt like something touched me on the side of the leg. It was just below my knee. I was feeling something on my leg." She turned to Scott and Louise. "Robin will come back and give you a report on her findings. But one thing that I found helps is that you'll have energies or spirits that don't necessarily know they're spirits. They don't know why we don't pay attention to them and don't know who you are, and so you're in their space. And time—time is really only a concept for the living. So get their attention by saying you love this house, you love this space. You want to make it a home. You want to improve it. I've moved into homes where there was an energy, and . . . they're afraid of us. That tension will build up, and it's like it gets upset, and you get upset—back and forth. So it's best to say, 'Hey, I love this space. I'm happy here.'"

We wrapped the session, packed up our gear, and headed out. Before departing, Maya and I discussed how to properly cleanse a house by smudging it with sage and suggested Louise do it daily for a while, decreasing the frequency slowly over time to once a week, and finally once a month.

The Evidence

Below is an excerpt from the evidence file. This evidence was recorded on the audio recorder that was placed in the rear bedroom/workroom before Scott and Louise returned. The group's self-proclaimed medium, Maya is kept in the dark about any of the details of an investigation so that she can go in with an open mind. I've sometimes found her to be eerily spot on and other times to be far off the mark. In this case, at twenty minutes in on the recording, she said something very interesting.

19:59 EMF spike at 4.0 on Maya's gauge while she and Brian do a round in the back bedrooms. Robin is at the surveillance cameras.

20:43 Maya asks, "You like the crawl space, huh?" Recall that Scott had reported to me that Louise would spend hours in the attic, despite the extreme heat, and would often act oddly up there. I had purposely not shared any of that information with Maya.

21:59 We depart the house to take a break when suddenly Maya gets very unusual EMF spikes in the back yard in a 100-yard radius of the house. Team spends several minutes outside exploring the area.

39:40 EVP of a female whispering, "Yes."

40:00 Maya reports having "major chills."

45:28 EMF spike of a 9.4 at the spot where Scott reported often seeing the apparition of the woman in the back hallway by the two bedroom doors.

46:48 Indistinguishable whispering.

51:58 Maya has a 9.4 EMF spike in hall; Robin's detector in the room is a 0.

52:00 Maya reports EMF spikes of 0.9 and 0.4. (The hallway and bathroom lights had been turned off when the team discovered during setup that they registered on our EMF gauges when on.)

53:46 Maya reports chills.

Throughout the night, not so much as a bug landed in the flour on the table. There wasn't a mark, a scratch, a fingerprint—nothing showed up in the flour. We also captured no shadowy entities poking their heads around corners. We did get a short EVP with a male voice responding to the question "Is Wilhelm here?" with a short but definitive "no." So it was impossible to say if the entity wasn't Wilhelm or if it was Wilhelm being difficult.

But we did record several EVPs by what sounds like an adult female. In one very clear EVP, we could hear her say, "In crystal." We had no idea what this meant, but the EVP was very distinct.

Then, in two separate and remarkable EVPs, the same female entity seems to repeat the same message twice:

First EVP. Indistinguishable whispering and then, "I can't see. Here, but seen in the eye before. Can't go out again. It's been five months in Delaware."

Second EVP. Again some indistinguishable whispering and then clearly, "In the eye before. I can't see. Didn't go out again. It's been five months alone."

Final Assessment

The two EVPs described above are the most remarkable and haunting EVPs of my career, for a number of reasons. First, the two EVPs are exceptional for their sheer length. Most EVPs are whispered one-or-two-word phrases. These were several sentences in length. They were also extremely similar in message, almost as if the entity were repeating a personal mantra, explaining to herself why she could not go out again. I wondered if the reason she couldn't leave was because she was blind or if she saw everything in the material world as somewhat hazy. I've often speculated that for spirits, the world at large appears very murky and that they have as much difficulty communicating with us as we do with them. Whether this is because they exist in a kind of semiconscious state or whether it's because our physical makeups are so different, I'm not certain. I have concluded that clear, concise communication between the two worlds seems difficult at best on both sides of the veil.

I did wonder why she felt trapped in the house, unable to leave. Was it some type of personal seclusion, which is what the EVPs suggested, or had she been held against her will? Was it the fact that she had been there so long that she now felt it necessary simply to stay, or so she tried to convince herself? Why couldn't she see, and why did she allude twice to something in her eye?

We started the investigation thinking we would find Wilhelm, and instead we found a woman who felt trapped within the confines of the Long Neck house. It was just another of those mysteries that seem to shroud anything to do with the paranormal.

A third EVP we captured was again a female voice rasping out what sounded like "*markssss.*" Honestly, until this moment in time, I hadn't thought much of the EVP, as it didn't really seem to pertain to anything. But then an awful thought crossed my mind. Perhaps the "marks" were on her body. Did she have marks either from abuse or self-harm? Perhaps this was why she no longer felt she could leave; perhaps the marks would give her away.

Was the voice we heard the older woman? The child? It sounded distinctly to me to be that of a young woman. In fact, we captured no EVPs that sounded like a small child at all that night, nor did we come across any evidence, such as marks in the flour or elsewhere, that evening to suggest a child spirit.

Near the very end of the evening, as we were wrapping up the combined session with Louise and Scott, Maya was walking about with her EMF detector in the family room when we caught a curiously clear EVP. Again a soft female voice implored, "You can leave now." I think perhaps we had exhausted her resources for the evening.

Postscript

I met with a calmer Scott and Louise for a post-investigation interview for the writing of this book. They admitted that they were both slightly reluctant to meet with me again. There had been no activity in the house for months, and construction was nearing completion. They weren't sure meeting with me wouldn't stir things up again. After the burning of the chair, the couple had very meticulously hunted every item that had belonged to Wilhelm and had either thrown it away or burned it. Louise had also very carefully followed Maya's instructions to ritually cleanse the dwelling with sage. The house was calm now, peaceful. Why jinx it? But after a few emails back and forth, they agreed to fill me in on events both past and present.

Now able to look at the situation much more rationally, Scott admitted that the worst of the activity had happened as soon as Louise left to visit family in California, as if the male spirit were targeting Scott in particular. "I don't think it wanted me to finish the house."

But after burning the chair and having the house blessed, Scott never again had the odd episodes. The rages, the passing out for long periods, the strange physical maladies, the big handprints—all of what seemed like Wilhelm's manipulations—all ceased.

The woman and the child spirit remained longer in the house, although they apparently were forced to vacate eventually, either due to the frequent cleansings or merely due to Louise's actions in the cleansing ritual, which indicated that their presence in the house was not welcome.

The Victorian woman departed a month or so after our investigation, and when she did, she made her displeasure known to Scott quite plainly. He got into his father's truck one day, closed the door, and glanced into the rearview mirror. There, sitting in the back seat, was the woman of the high cheekbones and serious mien staring back at him. He immediately turned around to look into the back seat, but she was not there. He turned back to look again at the rearview mirror, but no woman. As she had never seemed to interact with him when he saw her in the house, I asked him how she had acted when he saw her in the car.

"She wasn't looking out the window or anything. She was looking right at me. And she didn't have a happy face on. She seemed like one of those women who said, 'You better do it my way.' She might have been a strict mother or grandmother... very stern." That was the last time he saw her either in the house or on the property. It was almost as if she showed herself to Scott in the car as a way to acknowledge that the couple had won and she had vacated the property but that she wasn't happy with the situation.

But while it seemed the lady in the Victorian garb and Wilhelm had both departed, the child spirit seemed to linger for some time in the home. "We would have little pictures, drawn by little fingers.

More pictures of alligators, someone drowning, crudely drawn, like the drawings of a six-year-old. The alligator images might be a type of symbol of danger in the water, though Delaware is too far north to have alligators."

The images of drowning are also interesting. Scott confided to me that while alone with my investigator Maya, she had mentioned to him that she felt the child spirit was that of a six-year-old female who had drowned. Maya, who is by her own admission sensitive, has been asked not to give her opinions on such matters until the evidence has been reviewed. Apparently, she felt compelled in this case to make this claim to Scott. He admitted she had asked him to keep it to himself.

Scott continued, "I felt fingers moving on my legs all the time." He demonstrated by moving his fingers up and down his lower leg from ankle to knee. This would occur all over the house, but in particular in the back-left bedroom—coincidentally, the same bedroom where Louise had painted the pictures.

After the investigation was over, a large cabinet with tools was removed from the dining room, baring a large blank temporary wall. The footers for an adjoining family room area were poured, but construction had not begun on this section of the house. In the interim, a piece of drywall had been installed temporarily over what would someday be the walkway between the two rooms. Just for fun, Louise had taken a marker and drawn a smiley face on the raw drywall one day. She thought it would be cute, and apparently the child apparition thought it fun as well.

"For the next several months, all over the house were smiley faces drawn with a finger. In the dust, in the dog hair, on the TV screen, on the windows—there were smiley faces everywhere," Scott said. He even picked up a mattress that was lying on the floor in the back bedroom to find a smiley face drawn underneath. "And

I would ask Louise, did you do this? She'd say no. And I would say, well I didn't do it either. I think that she was mocking us."

Louise chimed in, "So one day he decided to paint over it."

"I didn't just paint over it. I sanded it off the drywall, because the paint wouldn't cover it."

Scott recalled a strange episode in the shower one morning. "I was in the shower, and, you know, the water hits you and splashes down. This morning it was hitting me and splashing two ways." Scott demonstrated with his hands that the stream of water was dividing in a V-shaped pattern. "And the shower curtain kept blowing and moving. And we didn't have the heat or air on. And I said, 'Come on, can't I get a shower by myself?' When I opened the shower curtain, there were already little wet footprints walking out on the rug and the tiles. I hadn't gotten out yet, and Louise was still sleeping. I had seen the shower curtain move, but not really open. But does the shower curtain really have to open for someone to get into or out of the shower?"

Then one day the couple was sitting on the couch making up when the front door opened. Scott described it: "The front door just opened, like ten, twelve inches. And it's latched—it's latched right now—I would never have a door that didn't latch by itself. So it unlatched, opened just wide enough for something to walk out, and then it closed. Why would it blow open ten inches? Why, if the wind blew it open, wouldn't it blow open all the way? It just opened this much and then *click*. Never felt anything in here, saw anything in here, never any designs anymore."

It appeared that the door opening and closing was the final scene for the ghost child. She heralded her departure from the house with her final supernatural feat. Louise concurred that the door opened and closed, and that was the last she time she'd ever had experiences in the home.

Post Postscript: "They live outside now."

Our investigator Brian left on a trip not long after we wrapped the investigation. Sitting next to him was a woman he did not know but who, it appeared in retrospect, had a message for him. They were conversing with some light banter during the flight, and the woman asked him what he had been doing in his free time. He hedged at first, not wanting to admit that he was a paranormal investigator. The woman seemed to be determined, however, and continued to ask pointed questions about his hobbies. He admitted that he'd done some undefined work for a couple and that the work involved a house. Finally, she asked what work he did, and he was cornered into admitting that he had done an investigation with a paranormal team at a house that involved a couple. Satisfied, the woman delivered the message that she had wanted him to know. "They live outside now," she said.

Brian was dumbfounded. Where had this information come from? Obviously, the woman was a rather powerful medium.

My final interview with Scott and Louise indicated that the message the woman on the plane had delivered to Brian appeared to be true. When I relayed the story to Scott and Louise, they were dumbfounded.

Louise's first words were an astonished "She said what? 'They live outside now'?"

Then the couple agreed with the summation. The Victorian woman had been seen one final time, in Scott's rearview mirror. She had never again been seen inside the house. And the child spirit appeared to unlatch and open the storm door, as if departing.

Now the couple reported that they often found markings on the outer side of the windows. The new master bedroom Louise had built has vaulted ceilings with windows placed at ceiling height. These would be approximately thirteen to fifteen feet above the ground outside. The couple reported finger marks appearing on the glass where someone simply couldn't be standing unless on a ladder. The finger marks worried Scott, who would grab a ladder and carefully wash the windows. A few days later, inexplicably, he'd find fingerprints again on the windows.

The hardest part of the couple's turmoil was the emotional drain and strain that it caused them. Even now when no paranormal activity was occurring in the house, Scott admitted that at the time he felt as if he was going crazy.

"When this was all going on, I thought I was going nuts," he said. "So I was so glad you guys came out here and found something. Because at first, I couldn't get Louise to believe me. But then she started seeing all the pictures in the couches. You can't fake that. That's why I would run over to my dad to show him. And he would say, 'Okay, let's brush it off, and we'll go for a little bit.' And we would come back and it was there."

Despite the fact that there hadn't been any paranormal activity in the home for many months, Louise had listed the house for sale but then had taken it off the market. Pressed for an explanation for why she had considered selling the house, after nearly all the renovations were completed and the difficulties were behind her, she said that the house itself had exacted too high a price in pain and emotional strain. "But, I'll probably keep it now," she added. "It's cost me so much."

CHAPTER 4
HAUNTED HOTEL
Berlin, Maryland

Located only six miles west of Ocean City, the quaint little historic town of Berlin, Maryland, is full of antique shops, artisans, and fabulous restaurants. As is the way of things, the actual name *Berlin* was not to honor German immigrants in the area but an accident of translation. The town was actually named for a well-to-do farmer by the name of Burleigh who owned much of the land in the area. After a minor mispronunciation of Burleigh, the borough became forever onward Berlin.

The town itself developed along a railroad line that brought salesmen and delivered livestock to the area. A devastating fire destroyed much of the timber structures in the town. It was therefore decreed by the town's mayor and councilmen in 1895 that all public buildings constructed in downtown Berlin would henceforward be constructed of brick. In retrospect it was a very astute decision as two later fires, in 1901 and 1904, again destroyed much of the town.

It was at the very center of town, therefore, that Horace Harmonson, the original owner and builder of the Atlantic Hotel, constructed the large three-story red brick inn, complete with balconies and a large front porch. The gracious three-story building became the very heart of the little town.

Indeed, when the telephone was invented, the hotel housed the only switchboard for most of Worcester County and the eastern shore. The switchboard itself was housed in what is today the dining room. The traveling salesmen in the area used the telephone service to send in their orders and communicate with their companies.

Originally, the hotel was built as a place for the steady stream of salesmen to pass a night as they got off the train and headed out to sell their wares all along the shore. These traveling salesmen were known as *drummers*. In the early nineteenth century, these door-to-door salesmen traversed the countryside with trunks full of goods and catalogs of their products, trying to sell their wares in the more remote areas of the countryside. The origin of the term *drummer* is not clear. It may have been coined in recognition that these salesmen were trying to "drum up" business, or it may have alluded to the large trunks or drums they hauled along with them. Either way, the term stuck. At the Atlantic Hotel, the restaurant and bar area is named Drummer's Café in honor of these salesmen.

Harmonson was apparently a shrewd businessman. He provided a horse-drawn bus that ran between the railroad and the hotel and ran a livery stable behind the hotel. Horses and mules that arrived by rail were driven up through town to the livery stable. The drummers could likewise hire a horse and buggy from Harmonson's stable in order to sell their wares. Sometimes the drummers came by horse, in which case Harmonson would purchase the winded, tired animal from the drummer and then sell him another at a higher price. He'd keep the purchased animals, rest them and feed them, and then sell them to another salesman or use the animals to pull the bus.

Harmonson ran the family's livery service, transporting the drummers, and the selling of the livestock, while his wife, Virginia, actually oversaw the day-to-day operation of the hotel.

Apparently, the hotel flourished with a constant stream of guests. Given that the vast majority of the guests at the hotel were male, it is not surprising that prostitutes also frequented the building. It is believed that one successful working lady may actually have resided on the property, purportedly in the Anna Suite, while she provided her services to the peddlers that frequented the establishment. At least one picture of the hotel's professional women adorns the wall in the lobby of the hotel, a testament to the hotel's immoral history. As beautiful as the building was, it had a colorful past complete with prostitutes, gambling, and at least one shooting.

Historic Berlin

The Atlantic Hotel is not the only aging mausoleum in Berlin. Its next-door neighbor the Pal building was built in 1895, and on the other side is a three-story brick building belonging to the Eternal Order of Oddfellows, which was built around the same time. All the historic brick buildings are now listed on the National Historic Registry.

The town saw a devastating economic downturn in the 1970s. The aging buildings became the haunts of derelicts and drug dealers. Many of the structures became run-down and were boarded up and all but abandoned. The hotel itself became a boarding house, a home to less desirable tenants who tended not to pay their rent. For a sad time in history, Berlin became a place to avoid instead of visit. In the wake of this, ten forward-thinking businesspeople decided that a change was needed. The courageous ten raised a million dollars to save the hotel, which had been the heart of the town for so long, in the hopes that in saving it, they'd save the rest of the town.

They purchased the old Atlantic Hotel in 1989 and renovated the structure, bringing it back to its original Victorian glory. They filled every room with period antiques and fine linens. They modernized the structure so that each room had a private bath, many still boasting the old ball and claw iron bathtubs. Rockers were placed on the front porch so guests could watch the comings and goings of tourists and locals as they strolled by on the cobbled sidewalks. They replaced the '70s chandeliers in the grand ballroom with the original crystal chandeliers, the gas lights converted to electricity.

The owners' gamble paid off. The renovation of the hotel sparked a renaissance not only for the hotel but for the whole town, which once again has a flourishing tourist trade. But while the derelicts are now gone, not all the hotel's residents have departed quite so congenially.

The Backstory

It didn't take the team long to research the claims of paranormal activity. The haunted history of the Atlantic Hotel is as highly publicized as the hotel itself. There are articles and blog posts aplenty. The hotel's haunts have also made it into books about East Coast hauntings, and it's a popular stop for the local ghost walking tour. Most of the stories are the stuff of urban legends now, having been retold and exaggerated for so long.

The front desk, which is right off the ballroom, has often been featured in articles, as it seemed to be a location of frequent activity, or so the reports indicated. The clerks that staff the office reported being the unwitting victims of ghostly pranks. Sometimes the adding machine seemed to take on a life of its own. It would start adding numbers, paper tape rolling, when there was no one operating it. Lights would suddenly turn off, leaving the clerk in the dark to flounder for the light switch. This never happened, however, when a guest was waiting for service, but only when the clerk was alone in the room. In the spirit of commerce, perhaps business was not to be interrupted.

The ballroom also had a haunted reputation. Supposedly, ghostly piano music was sometimes reported when there was no one at the aging keyboards. Staff often reported feeling a presence in the room.

One of the most well-known legends about the place is the death of a little girl who supposedly fell out a window in one of the corner rooms of the second floor. The hotel's most famous ghost is that of the little sprite, who is now believed to haunt the second floor. Guests and staff have reported hearing the sounds of childish giggles and what is theorized to be the sounds of a tricycle being ridden up and down the hall.

After working alone late one night, a night clerk, Barbara, reported distinctly hearing what sounded like something being moved across the floor above her. She went up to the second floor to investigate the noise but found nothing out of the ordinary. It happened several more times. Barbara would hear the noise of something being moved from one end of the hall to the other, but upon investigating the noise, could never find the source. She finally brought the topic up with another employee of the hotel, who said that they believed it was the sound of the little girl ghost riding her tricycle.

Staff members, especially those who worked the night shift, reported hearing things like footsteps in the hall, especially on nights when they were closing up and no one else was around. And some reported seeing shadowy figures in the second-floor hall.

The grand staircase right off the ballroom had also seen its share of publicity. It is the spot of one of the most preposterous stories about the hotel—an urban legend right out of *Poltergeist*. According to the story, a staff member was one day ascending the stairs from the first floor to the second floor in order to retrieve some supplies. As she approached the first-floor landing, a pair of swinging doors that lead out to a covered porch slowly opened and stayed opened. She stopped. When she resumed walking, the doors slowly closed and stayed closed. She retrieved her supplies from the second floor and headed back down the stairs, only to find that all the pictures on the stairway had been tilted and now hung askew. How was that possible? she wondered. She'd only been upstairs for a few minutes.

Infamous Room 16

On the second floor, Room 16 is probably the most famous room for haunted activity. The world's tiniest hotel room has a gargantuan reputation. One tall tale leads back to the renovation of the hotel and recounts the moving pictures in the room. Apparently, at the end of the renovations, the staff were pressed to put the finishing touches on the rooms, lining the drawers with paper and hanging pictures and the like.

While changing the paper liners in the drawers in Room 16, a staffer found a small silhouette of George Washington in one of the drawers. They hadn't yet decided where pictures were to be hung, so the staffer placed the silhouette upright on the dresser. A week later, she was placing blow dryers in the dresser drawers of all the rooms. She found a picture in a drawer in a different room, this one a small framed photo of a little girl in a blue dress. It hadn't been in the drawer a week before when she was changing out the paper. No one admitted to having put it there. She was perplexed.

She decided that the picture of the girl would be better in Room 16 than the George Washington silhouette, so she went into the room to switch the two pictures out. But the silhouette was no longer on the dresser where the staffer had left it. Instead, it was now hanging on the wall. She asked around. No one admitted to hanging the picture. The mystery was never solved. The picture of the little girl in the blue dress still hangs next to the dresser in Room 16.

Some appear to believe that the child ghost once resided in Room 16 of the hotel. It wasn't unusual for servants to live in a small room on the premises of their employer. In fact, a 1910 census for the hotel lists eight such boarders. Servants would have lived in small rooms tucked out of the way of the guests. Room 16 is one such room. It's actually located down a short hallway off the main hallway and is very small, so small it lacks even a closet. It's also located directly over the kitchen, so it's not prime real estate from the hotel's standpoint. It would have made a perfect room for a servant, one who might have brought a child. Perhaps the servant brought a child she couldn't watch during the day because she was working. Perhaps the child inadvertently fell out a window and died—a child who came but never left.

Room 16 is home to the phantom hotel guest as well. During one incident, the general manager was walking down the second-floor hallway when she was stopped by an irate guest who came out of Room 16. The woman asked the manager, "Do you work here?" to which the manager replied, "Yes, what can I do to help you?"

The lady said, "There are no towels in my room."

The manager was confused. For one thing, she had no recollection of seeing this guest, and she usually knew every guest who checked in. "How many towels do you need?" the manager inquired, thinking perhaps more than one person was staying the room.

The mysterious woman replied, "I have *no* towels."

The manager was incredulous. How could her staff have prepared a room and not put any towels in it? She headed off to retrieve the linens. When she arrived back at Room 16, she found the door ajar. She knocked on the door anyway, not wishing to startle the woman by simply appearing in the room. Oddly, she got no answer. The door being slightly open, the manager stuck her head into the room and called out for the woman, but still got no answer.

Thinking perhaps the woman was in the bathroom, the manager called out loudly, "Ma'am, I have your towels. Do you want me to put them on the bed?" Still she heard nothing.

She decided to try knocking again, but before she could get out the first rap, the door to the room flew open of its own accord. From her vantage point at the door, the manager saw that the bathroom door was open and that no one was in either the bathroom or the bedroom and that indeed the bathroom was fully stocked with towels. Now thoroughly perplexed, the manager went down to the lobby to inquire who was staying in Room 16. The clerk informed her that there was no one staying in the room.

While guests of the hotel often report experiencing paranormal activity, it's workers in the building, especially the maintenance staff, who report being the most often targeted recipients of unwanted attention. There are numerous reports of maintenance people being tapped on the shoulder by unseen hands, having their tools disappear, and being locked in spaces unwittingly. One contractor in particular told the story of the time he lost a paint scraper in Room 24. He'd had it one moment, and the next it was gone. He looked everywhere for the missing tool but couldn't find it. He finally gave up and went downstairs to get another one. He arrived back at the room only to find his paint scraper standing straight up on its end in the middle of the room. After that, the workman refused to work in Room 24.

The Initial Walk-Through

Renne, Gene, and I arrived at the Atlantic Hotel on a Saturday afternoon for the initial walk-through. Our interest piqued, we'd read the myriad articles on the hotel's hauntings and also researched the long and colorful past of the structure and the town. Would the old building prove to be as interesting as its reputation? It was an extraordinary day indeed. It was the middle of February, yet the temperature was unbelievably in the 70s. It was a little glimpse of spring and it wouldn't last. Apparently, everyone had decided to celebrate the lovely day, because we arrived in Berlin to find the town thronged with both tourists and locals. In fact, we had some difficulty driving down Main Street with all the foot traffic, let alone finding a place to park. It appeared that the streets of Berlin weren't actually intended for vehicle traffic, as everywhere there were kids riding skateboards or bicycles and people walking. The gift shops and local candy shop were likewise thronged.

We finally arrived at the Atlantic Hotel and found it was every bit as charming as its description. We were meeting with Matt, the maintenance manager, who had worked at the hotel for a number of years and who had grown up and lived in or around Berlin all his life. Matt was also Renne's son-in-law. It had been Matt who had negotiated with the manager to allow us to investigate the hotel and to work out the terms of the investigation.

It quickly became apparent that Matt, a gregarious young man, seemed to know everyone in Berlin intimately. As we stood in the back parking lot making his acquaintance, he chatted up the kitchen staff and said hello to the town's microbrewery owner, who arrived by bicycle and looked like a grunge rock musician from the '90s despite his business acumen. The brewer was headed over to the art shop he'd just opened across the street. He'd just wanted to park his bike at the hotel.

Matt, who had an intimate knowledge of the Atlantic Hotel, would be our tour guide that day. Once Renne, Gene, and I had assembled, Matt led us inside. Despite a modern-looking elevator right off the back door, an eyesore left over from the '70s, everything else in the building, from the custom draperies to the old front desk, gave the illusion that we'd just stepped into the past.

The place was humming with activity. Waiters and bussers worked furiously, hauling entrees from the kitchen to the dining room. The clerk at the front desk was fielding calls and handing out keys on brass key rings.

Matt stopped outside the ballroom to point out an old menu from 1914 mounted in a frame and now adorning the wall. The executive chef often tried to duplicate dishes from the time period using the menu as his guide, Matt informed us. The lobster salad sounded wonderful, but Matt admitted that the turtle soup wasn't his favorite.

The hotel is lovely at any season, Matt said, but it's at its best during the holidays. "It's beautiful at Christmas; it's like Charles Dickens Land. We celebrate everything in Berlin. Like, little Bobby got an A on his report card, and we shut down the streets—there's beer, everybody parties. It's awesome. There's no crime. I don't even lock my car. All the hood rats, we employ all of them."

We went into the grand ballroom first, the room of the phantom piano music. It was small by modern standards but elegant, boasting high ceilings with crown moldings and the famous crystal chandeliers. The space had been enlarged during the hotel's renovation when the owners combined an old billiards room with the ballroom. According to Matt, "Everything in here is old, heavy, and expensive. There are no reproductions; it's all the original stuff."

Matt reported that personally he'd had the most experiences in the ballroom. "They don't like it when we mess with or change stuff," he said. "I've experienced the most in these rooms. Temperature changes, hair on your neck [standing up]. And I won't even be thinking about it. I'm doing other things, and it happens." Matt reiterated the story of the ghostly piano music. Patrons had reportedly informed him of times that they'd heard the sound of piano music, seemingly coming from the ballroom. There was an old piano in the ballroom area that looked like it hadn't been played in years. I walked over to the instrument and pushed back the broken wooden lid and plunked a couple of notes on its decrepit keyboard, only to ascertain that the instrument hadn't been maintained nor tuned for some time. Of the ballroom, Matt commented, "We have had a lot of weddings in here and a lot of funerals. So a lot of happy things and a lot of sadness."

All the furniture in the hotel, Matt informed us, was period correct. The floors were the original hardwood, adorned with Persian rugs. Well preserved, all of the antiques are still in use in the hotel. The oldest piece of furniture resided in Room 11, an armoire that was simply too large to move when the renovations began. The contractors had to renovate around the leviathan when the upgrades were made.

Across the hall from the ballroom was the restaurant and bar, Drummer's. Matt recalled a personal experience he had while shutting the restaurant down one evening. One of his responsibilities was to straighten all the pictures on the walls before leaving at night, especially in the dining room, which was the most inhabited room of the building. On this particular night, he straightened the pictures and then locked up. Being such an integral part of the running of the hotel, he was often the last of the staff to leave at night and the first one to arrive in the morning. The next day, he arrived at the restaurant, unlocked the door, and entered the dining room, only to find that all the pictures on the far wall had been tilted to the right and now were hanging crookedly at an angle.

We noticed that old pictures adorned all the walls: prints, black and white photos, and paintings. All the walls were adorned with antique artwork. Matt informed us that the photos in particular were original to the area. If they weren't original to the building, he assured us, then they were from the closely surrounding region.

Matt next led us to the grand staircase, the one with the opening doors and the moving pictures. The staircase had an especially fine display of old photographs. Past tourneys and town events were pictured as were portraits and group photos of former residents. All the photos spoke of the town's colorful history. Included in the menagerie was a photo of Horace Harmonson and his wife, Virginia.

We started asking questions and exploring immediately, the claims of activity being rather preposterous. We found quickly that the two glass doors on the landing of the grand staircase swung quite easily and would open when a vacuum was created by the door to the outdoor porch being opened. It was fathomable that the doors opening and closing on their own could have happened naturally. But what about all the pictures being tilted? There were a lot of pictures hung on the wall. When we asked a couple of front desk staff about the story, we quickly found that the answer was much more prosaic.

The front desk clerk who'd experienced the phenomena on the grand staircase, Antonia, happened to be on duty that day. She graciously clarified for us what actually happened, which was significantly less exciting than the rumors. She had been walking up the stairs as the original story had claimed. The doors did open and stay open, just as had been reported. However, she clarified that there was no wind that day and that she couldn't account for why the two doors had swung open so oddly. She had gone up, she said, to check the coffee station on the second floor, and when she came back down, one very specific picture, not all, was tilted: a photograph of a young woman in a white dress who had been a member of the Hammond family, the family that ran the hotel after the Harmonsons.

The old photograph in question hung at around shoulder height on the staircase. Now, it's certainly not out of the realm of the plausible that someone walking up the stairs, possibly carrying heavy baggage, might have hit one of the pictures on the wall, causing it to tilt. However, Antonia was careful to demonstrate that the photograph in question was actually hung on two hooks, making it less likely to move. An examination of the back of the photograph revealed the words *Property of Ed Hammond.*

Another employee of the hotel confirmed that she had also come down the stairs to find that particular photograph tilted on its side on a different occasion.

As I said before, it seemed possible that someone dragging up a large suitcase could bump into the photograph and thus change its position despite its two hooks. But the story had now become one of the legends that surrounded the old hotel, kept alive by staff who quite obviously loved the old building and its quirky happenings.

With Matt in tow, we ascended to the second floor, which the child ghost was reputed to haunt. About the legends of the second floor, Matt admitted that witnesses sometimes reported seeing a figure looking out the windows of corner rooms that had no guests booked for the night. There didn't appear to be a pronounced pattern to these sightings, and they happened in different rooms. "I've seen it sometimes," Matt admitted. "I thought I saw something, but I couldn't be sure. You look again, and there's nothing there."

It's believed that the ghosts of children are usually much more interactive, unlike their adult counterparts, who may try to avoid places that are inhabited and stick to quiet spaces where they can reside in peace. This certainly seemed to be the case with the child ghost on the second floor. Our team did some research into the claim of a child dying by falling. Police records didn't go back that far, nor did the local paper. We were unable to verify the validity of the story.

Staff often reported hearing the sound not only of a tricycle being ridden but also of a ball being bounced. Guests who were strangers to the hotel also reported hearing a tricycle or laughing. The front desk manager noted that often if the staff received a report from one guest about their experience, they'd usually get two or three from other guests who said they'd heard the same thing.

A childish giggle was also amongst the frequent reports. The manager, Natalie, said that just a couple of weeks before we'd arrived for the walk-through, two separate couples had come down to the front desk and asked if there was a small child in the hotel. Both couples had reported hearing giggling in the hall very late at night. Natalie told them that children weren't allowed to stay in the hotel, and that the night before there had been no children in the building. She asked if the giggling had been loud. Both couples noted that the giggles had been quiet but distinct, distinct enough to be reported the next day. The fact that multiple guests, often guests who had no knowledge of the hotel's haunted reputation, reported the same phenomena increased the credibility of the reports, as did the reporting of childish noises in a building where children cannot stay.

A couple staying in Room 20 had recently reported odd activity, Matt informed us. The couple was awakened in the middle of the night when the lights in their room suddenly came on. The woman was scared and wanted to leave, but it was the middle of the night and, besides, she reasoned, nothing sinister had happened. So they turned off the lights and went back to sleep. In the morning, her husband couldn't find the cap to his Tylenol bottle. He had taken a couple of Tylenol before going to sleep the night before and had placed the bottle and the lid on the bedside table. The man reported that he'd looked everywhere for the lid, even going so far as to tear apart the bed in search of it. It just simply was not to be found. Housekeeping did not find the lid either when cleaning the room.

While the team was investigating the hotel, we caught an unsolicited story from one of the hotel guests. Apparently, this particular guest had lived in Berlin all her life and was well versed with the stories. She took one look at our surveillance cameras and audio recorders and explained it to her friend. It appeared she knew that we were there to conduct a paranormal investigation, and we hadn't been the only team to do so over the years. She admitted that everyone in town knew of the hotel's haunted reputation. Then she explained her own family history with the spirits. An aunt of hers had been a caregiver to a long-time resident of the hotel and would come and go frequently to see her patient who lived on the second floor. Aunt Marie told her niece that she would exit her patient's room and come out into the hallway and see ghosts.

Matt led us to Room 16, another haunt of the child ghost. Matt spoke of his own experiences in the room. "Sometimes when I'm working in the bathroom, working on the drain or something, it will feel like someone is sitting on me."

Room 22 on the second floor had a bad reputation. Apparently, someone was shot in a card game gone bad sometime around 1900. We couldn't get into Room 22 that day, nor the night of the investigation, as other guests had booked the room. Room 23 also had a reputation among staff members as being the room where the door would slam shut. The staffer would be in the room straightening up, plumping the pillows and the like, with the door to the hall standing open. Having finished their task, they'd walk toward the door to exit the room only to have it slam shut in their face. This happened with some frequency. Unfortunately, Room 23 was likewise occupied.

Having seen what we could on the second floor, we ascended to the third floor. While the second floor was the center of the most activity, Matt noted that the "third floor was just creepy. You get vertigo." It became quickly apparent what he meant. The aged floors on the third-floor hallway had sunken dramatically in the center with age. The unevenness made for a very unsteady walk down the hall, which may be part of the uneasiness people felt. The third floor was also darker, with only the heavily curtained windows on either end of the hallway to provide natural light. The third floor felt out of the way, as if time had forgotten it. Few guests booked rooms up this high. On this particular day, there was absolutely no one about on the third floor. Matt took us directly across the hall to the Anna Suite, which was reportedly haunted by the spirit of a prostitute who had once lived there. While Room 16 and the second-floor hallway were the locations most often cited as being haunted, Matt said that it was truly the Anna Suite where employees in particular felt the most uneasy.

As we approached the door of the suite, the otherwise genial Matt started to act distinctly uneasy. He had trouble with the lock on the door. He tried it a couple of times and then looked around at us. "That never happens," he said. He tried the lock again but couldn't get it open. He then threw his hands up in the air and announced, "I'm out of here. I'm not messing with it."

If we hadn't been waiting for him to show us the suite, I believe Matt would have walked away without entering. A few moments later, he collected himself and decided to try the lock one more time. Finally, the old lock cooperated, and Matt was able to open the door, though he was still hesitant to cross the threshold. He sidled out into the hallway as the three of us entered the suite. "Enjoy," called Matt from his position in the hall.

What we saw in the Anna Suite was hardly sinister. A lovely sitting room with an old wicker chair and couch resplendent with throw pillows met our gazes. Marble-top side tables and a coffee table with turned legs added a feeling of age. Old pictures and prints were hung on all the walls, and here too the light fixtures and lamps were antiques. A large buffet with an ornate mirror was situated along the inner wall. Period-style knickknacks and vintage tins rounded out the decor. It certainly seemed too airy a room to have caused so much consternation from our host.

Finally, Matt decided to throw caution to the wind and joined us in the sitting room. "I don't know why. I get a weird feeling in here. I just don't like this room," he reiterated.

"Hello, hi, it's me," he greeted whatever entities resided here, showing them respect. "Don't scare me," he added as he headed through the kitchen area to the bedroom.

I asked him what in particular made him so uncomfortable in the Anna Suite, and he replied, "It's everyone." He explained that "no one on the staff likes this room." He admitted to a feeling of dread and then recounted an amazing EVP that another paranormal group had captured in the Anna Suite during their investigation. In the chilling EVP, a female spirit voice had named all the staff members beginning with the owners and the manager and worked down the hierarchal list, as if to demonstrate that she knew who they all were. He'd asked the group to stop the recording before the voice said his name. He hadn't wanted to hear it.

Matt continued, "They named the owner and the general manager, and I just said, 'Stop. I'm next in the pecking order, and I don't want to hear this.'" The group had also reported hearing barking sounds from underneath the bed.

Certainly, an EVP that listed all the staff members by name would be extremely troubling, but I wondered if anything besides the spooky EVP caused him to be uneasy in the suite. He went on to explain that, for some unknown reason, he often felt sick in the rooms and couldn't remain in them for very long.

Matt said he often felt nauseous when in the Anna Suite, but that as soon as he walked across the threshold into the hall he felt fine. During our investigation, the team performed an EMF sweep of the suite. In a closet off the sitting room, we found a breaker box that was giving off extremely high EMF all along the inner wall where the buffet was located. High electromagnetic fields such as this can cause feelings of sickness, headaches, fatigue, and even hallucination with extended exposure. It may be that part of what Matt was experiencing when working in the room was due to the EMF fields.

Gene noted that adding to the weird feelings in the suite was the fact that the floor in the bedroom drooped quite notably toward the center of the building. To demonstrate, he placed a cylindrical shampoo bottle on the floor in the bathroom and we watched it immediately roll downhill under the sink. Again we suggested that feeling of vertigo, of being a little off-kilter, could contribute in part to the feelings of uneasiness in the suite.

Matt continued, "Now I can feel it on my chest. It's dread. I just don't like this room. Sometimes it's cold in here. You'll read the thermostat and it will say it's 70 in here, and yet it will feel like 50. I feel like they're just watching us right now."

"They probably are," Renne agreed. Renne has demonstrated a natural sensitivity on many of our investigations. While I don't use sensitives on the team per se and Renne has no formal training, she has proven herself a harbinger. She'd report feeling a chill or a touch, and then upon evidence review we'd find evidence to back up her experience. It's happened far too often for me to dismiss her feelings out of hand. I asked her, therefore, what she felt in the room and she hedged, admitting only that she had felt something…

"But the Anna is creepy," Matt again reiterated. He noted that a staff member we had met on the first floor didn't like the room either. "She wanted to see the ghost room. I took her and a couple of staff up there, and she was like, 'No, I don't want any part of this.' It's the people that I don't tell, and we'll be walking through, and they'll say, 'I don't want any part of this.' And I'll be watching them, and they'll be looking around. You can't fake scared. You can't fake scared. You can act scared, but you can't fake scared. So, I would watch them to see their reaction."

Matt then filled us in on the history of the room. According to the old stories, the suite of rooms was once inhabited by a successful prostitute around the late 1800s. In the first-floor hall, Matt informed us, there still hung a picture that showed the resident lady of the evening sitting on the ledge of an upper-story window. We later found the picture hanging on the wall near the front entrance to the hotel. Dressed in a white, frilly dress, a woman with her dark hair pulled back in one of the elaborate hairstyles of the era sat on the windowsill in a corner room of the third floor. I wondered if we had found our woman.

Matt continued that Christmastime was a quieter time for paranormal activity in the building. "Christmastime—it's very joyful around here. I hang Christmas lights in all the windows. You get a lot less of the feelings." Summertime, when all the rooms were rented every night, the staff rarely noticed any activity either, being far too busy perhaps to pay the spirits any attention.

The paranormal activity, however, usually spiked up after Christmas through around April. In other words, the slow, dreary months of winter when the hotel experienced its slowest season were when the staff noted the most activity. This wasn't surprising because when the hotel was quieter and the staff less harried with the demands of guests, they would be more in tune with the echoes of the past.

Matt finished his recounting of the hotel's hauntings by saying that while guests sometimes reported activity, it was really the staffers who reported the bulk of it, which we'd learned in our own perusal of the hotel's haunted reputation. Perhaps more significantly, it was the contractors the manager often hired to perform services who were the most often targeted by paranormal pranks.

A former banquet coordinator for the hotel was, according to Matt, a favored victim of the spirits. "They would deadbolt her into rooms. She was a really pretty young girl, and they would just play with her. She would have to call down to the office to help get her out. But she was cool with it. It didn't really bother her."

Matt continued, "But the guy that ran out of here—he was legitimately scared. That was the second week I worked here, and I was out in the parking lot." During a conversation, both Matt and the executive chef witnessed the painter decamping the premises with his hastily gathered equipment. Matt asked him where he was going in such a hurry. All he said was "goodbye."

Matt had said, "You can't go."

"No, I'm done," the painter had replied. "They took my paint, they took my brushes, they locked me in a room, and I'm out of here." At first Matt assumed it was someone on the staff who had been pranking the poor man. No one, however, would confess to the crime.

Apparently, the painter wasn't the only outside person to be targeted. "They don't like change. They don't like changing stuff," Matt concluded, explaining why contractors were so often the target.

After the tour of the Anna Suite, Matt led us back down to the first floor, the tour over. There we met the vivacious Pat, an elderly woman in her eighties, sitting in a chair by the front entrance. Pat now lived in the hotel on the second floor. Astonishingly, we found out that Pat was the great-granddaughter of Horace and Virginia Harmonson, the original owners of the Atlantic, which was why she was allowed the dispensation of living in the building. Pat, not surprisingly, loved the grand old hotel that had been a part of her family history for generations, but she staunchly dismissed the idea that the historic edifice was haunted. Indeed, what was remarkable was that she was the first person we had met all afternoon who didn't regale us with stories about their paranormal experiences in the building.

Pat, in fact, adamantly denied ever having seen or heard anything out of the ordinary and freely admitted that she didn't believe in ghosts. Renne, who appeared to take up an immediate affinity with the lady, offered to take Pat to lunch at a later date.

Wooed by a free meal and culinary contentment, Pat made some surprising admissions to Renne at their luncheon date, admissions that none of us saw coming, considering her vehement denial that the hotel was haunted. While she herself did not believe in ghosts, nor had she ever experienced anything in the building, Pat reiterated, other members of her family had not been of the same opinion.

Great-Grandfather Horace Harmonson himself had apparently had some uncomfortable incidents in the hotel that he had built. Late in life, and in declining health, Horace and Virginia had finally taken up residence in the hotel. This was presumably after the poker game shooting and the rumored child falling to her death from a window. When Horace finally did move into the building that he had built, he refused to sleep in Room 22, the room where the shooting had taken place. His granddaughter Sally also found this room frightening. Pat said that Sally reported that when she did sleep there, she would wrap her nightgown tightly around herself for protection. Her grandparents would often sleep with her in that room at night for comfort. Most of Pat's family reported hearing footsteps and strange noises in the building.

Horace Harmonson himself died in his beloved hotel on July 27, 1933, after battling a five-year illness. Confined to his bed for the last two weeks of his life, he died in his room on the second floor. He was seventy-three when he passed.

The Investigation

The team returned on a *very* cold, rather forlorn evening in March to do our investigation. If February had been uncharacteristically warm, March was proving to be extremely cold. It was, in short, one of those nights in deep winter when all the world appeared asleep, slumbering with their dreams until spring arrived and life began again. A perfect night, in essence, to search out the mysteries of the world, those just below the surface of our awareness.

Despite the enormity of the job, only the three investigators who had come on our initial walk-through returned for the investigation, all the other team members having begged off. Renne, Gene, and I arrived in the early evening to do a full night investigation in as many spaces as we could gain access to, determined to make the most of the situation. The hotel was running as usual that evening, and we found to our disappointment that many of the spaces we had hoped to investigate had been already booked. Neither Room 22 of the gambling game gone bad nor Room 23 were available. Renne had reserved Room 16, the room the child ghost was thought to inhabit. My husband, Gene, and I had decided to try our luck with the Anna Suite. We had permission to set up equipment in the hallway of the second floor where the sounds of tricycle riding, a ball bouncing, and a child giggling had all been reported.

Second-Story Hallway

We set up three IR-capable surveillance cameras in the hall on the second floor, one on either end of the long hall and the third facing down the short hallway to Room 16 and Pat's door. The hotel guests had not been apprised of the fact that a paranormal investigation was being conducted that evening even as they were staying in the hotel.

One guest in particular was very uncomfortable with the surveillance cameras recording her comings and goings, and she decided to rearrange the angles of the tripod-mounted cameras when we weren't looking, much to our chagrin. We tucked our digital video recorder (DVR) and monitor into the women's parlor alcove across from the grand staircase, such that anyone venturing past the draperies of the alcove could monitor the camera footage. Our same camera-moving guest would spend some time there that evening, sipping wine and viewing our footage. Such are the concessions one makes when trying to do an investigation in a working hotel.

Room 16

The tiniest hotel room on the planet, Room 16, was also one of the loveliest, with its majestic mahogany antique bed and original ball and claw tub. Given that the reported ghost was a little girl, I brought a Raggedy Ann doll as a trigger object, in hopes that our friend might try to play with it. Renne set up her IR-capable video recorder in the far corner by the bed, plugging it in so that it would record all night, or at least until its memory card was filled. In the shot of the bureau and the bathroom doorway was the small picture of the child who had been chronicled in articles of the hotel's hauntings. Despite the fact that the video camera also had audio, we placed an additional audio recorder and a data logger—a device that detects several different environmental factors and records the data.

Anna Suite

In the Anna Suite, we set up video cameras in both the sitting room and the bedroom. Another voice recorder and a data logger were placed on the bed in full view of the camera. Watching this particular sensor on the video camera throughout the night, I noted that the vibration meter did not go off when we opened and shut the bathroom door. The door to the bathroom was next to the bed, and it had a habit of sticking such that you really had to pull it open and shut.

In one piece of video, Gene came into the room and retrieved something from his coat pocket. He rummaged around in the pockets of the coat, which was lying on the bed, and at one point even moved the coat to another spot on the bed, but the vibration meter never registered movement. What piqued my interest was the fact that there was hardly anyone on the third floor that evening. There is a woman who lives in a room across the hall from the Anna Suite, on the third floor, but she was away for the weekend. All the guests, except for Gene and me, we carefully noted, were staying on the second floor. Yet several times throughout the night when the room was empty, the vibration sensor could be seen going off, as if someone or something was near the bed. If the third floor was mainly deserted and no one was in the room, what made the meter register vibration?

Also recorded in the room when it was deserted were two distinct footfalls, which was a phenomenon the staff reported hearing usually late at night when they were closing up.

We conducted a session in the sitting room and later the bedroom of the suite but really didn't seem to have much interaction. Renne did say she thought she felt something touch her ear while we were in the sitting room. With nothing else to back up personal experiences, however, it is my policy to disregard these more subjective observations.

Activity in the sitting room lacking, we moved to the bedroom. Honestly, the atmosphere in the bedroom felt different, more charged. My rods indicated an uptick in energy as well, I found, as I walked a circuit of the room, yet we were getting very little in the way of interaction. None of the meters registered any changes, and we hadn't had any personal experiences. We were actually starting to feel a bit bored. Renne and I sat down in the armchairs on either side of a small coffee table. I set my Mel Meter on the table so that I could read the display while conversing. With little else to do, we talked between ourselves about the horse show that Renne's granddaughter was attending that weekend.

Suddenly, the alarm on the Mel Meter blasted long and loudly, indicating a change in the electromagnetic field. So vehement a response was it that I startled and jumped out of my chair.

"Well, hello!" I exclaimed. "So you do want to talk." I'd had that this particular meter out on various investigations and never heard the alarm sound before, so I was rather shocked that it sounded so suddenly. Unfortunately, the meter didn't go off again the rest of the evening, upon request or otherwise.

I've noticed this often on investigations, this type of hide-and-seek response. When you're actively trying to interact with an entity, they play hard to get, taunting you with just a little something just out of range of your sight, or worse yet, going silent altogether. But when you stop paying attention to them, this is exactly when they decide they want said attention.

Second-Story Hallway

It was the hallway on the second floor where the team experienced the most activity. The claims of the sound of the little girl riding her tricycle gave me an idea. We hunted up a little red tricycle, complete with bell and streamers on the handlebars. We placed audio recorders and a REM Pod by the trike, hoping to attract the attention of something. It was when I was placing the REM Pod beside the tricycle that the alarm sounded vociferously, even after I had placed it on the floor and backed off. It went off one other time that evening, sounding just a short blast, when the team was heading down the stairs to conduct a session in the ballroom. All three of us heard the alarm. We immediately turned around and ran back up the stairs to the tricycle, thinking that one of the guests had been interfering with the equipment. Human contamination can be a factor, especially when in a public building. The hall was deserted, and no one, at least that we could see, was anywhere near the tricycle.

It was still early in the evening, and we had the hallway to ourselves. We were setting up the surveillance camera system. Renne decided to place her audio recorder at the end of the hall, nestled in a bookshelf away from prying eyes. She had just placed the recorder in the bookshelf and walked away when a whispery female voice was captured asking, "Can you hear me?" I especially liked this EVP because it was so obviously a clean recording. The recorder was hidden from view, and based on our recordings, it was clear there was no one near the recorder when the voice was caught.

We got the rest of the equipment set up and started with a session in the hallway. Immediately, we could tell that it was going to be an interesting session. I pulled out my rods to get a feel for the energy, and they went crazy, spinning in such wild circles that they were banging into one another and the furniture. I can only recall the rods reacting in such a violent manner on one other investigation. Unfortunately, they weren't reacting to my verbal requests for yes and no answers. Normally, I ask the rods to visibly cross for a yes answer or remain parallel for a no or neutral answer. They weren't having any of it. It was more as if whatever was making the rods spin was just so elated to visit with us that it just couldn't help itself.

As I said before, I don't present my dowsing rod sessions as evidence; they're more for my own information. However, the longer

I've worked with the rods, the more I've begun to trust their ability to measure the energy in an area. As the rods were spinning wildly, I experienced chills and tingling sensations, as did Renne, and then, beautifully, the Mel Meter that I had placed at my feet started registering changes in EMF where it had been a flat zero at the start. There were temperature changes also during the long nine minutes of interaction, but only of a couple degrees: the highest was 73.3 degrees Fahrenheit and the lowest was 72. We usually consider temperature fluctuations of 8 degrees or more to be significant.

During the session we also captured EVPs: one of whispering and another that sounded distinctly like a child giggling, in a hotel that doesn't allow children. This was a golden piece of evidence, as childish giggling was often reported by the staff and guests as well. A portion of the nine-minute transcript is below. I was counting on the idea that I had connected with the child ghost and thus was trying to connect with her by talking about things that a child would enjoy.

ROBIN: Can you do that again? Come up by me? I just got crazy chills. (*Reads EMF meter at her feet.*) We're at a 0.1. Can you do that again? Ewww (*reacting to the chills on her right side*). Tell me what your favorite game is, maybe we can play it... You like these rods now, don't you? You like spinning them? Did you ever have a pinwheel? You blow it and it spins... I had pinwheels too. (*The rods strike themselves together.*)... Crazy chills.[11]

---

11. I rather like to direct my EVP sessions in this way. Instead of asking random questions, I try to find a theme that might resonate with an entity, if I have some idea of who the entity might be. In this case, the ferocity of the spinning rods gave me an idea: connect the spinning rods to other childhood toys that spin. As I seemed to be having good results, both with personal experiences and with the uptick in the rods, I decided to continue on in that vein.

RENNE: I used to like to spin in the yard.

ROBIN: Yeah, I liked that too. Did you like to do that too? Did you ever stand in the middle of the yard and spin, spin, spin around? Spin around, spin around, and spin around until you fell down? (*Again the rods spin around so fast they are heard clearly in the audio.*) Did you ever do that? Do these rods remind you of that? Is that why you like to spin them so much?

RENNE: (*Reading the Mel Meter at her feet*) 0.1.

ROBIN: Spin, spin, spin till you (*whispering*) fall down ... It makes you so dizzy, doesn't it? Makes you so dizzy.

The rods spin fast and rhythmically.

ROBIN: Did you like the playground? On the merry-go-round? I like merry-go-rounds. I used to play on them every day on the playground.

RENNE: Hmm (*wiggles in her seat*), I just got the chill now.

ROBIN: 0.1, it is 0.1 by me ... 0.3. You are here now, aren't you? 0.2, 0.3, 0.2. So tell me about the merry-go-rounds. Is that your favorite thing? 0.2. Do you know what else I really like? I like carousels, with the pretty horses. Did you ever ride the ... 0.2 ... did you ever ride the carousel with the pretty horses? They go up and down. I always liked to ride the black ones. What was your favorite color?—0.1, 0.2?...Did you like the carousel? 0.1. Did you ever ride the carousel? 0.1. 74.1, 74.2, 73.9, 73.0.[12]

12. At this point I started to notice fluctuations in the temperature as well, so I started naming off the different degrees Fahrenheit that I witnessed.

ROBIN: Did you ever see a circus? (*The rods go wild banging into each other.*) 0.1, 73.0 … 0.2, 72.9. Did you ever go to the circus?… Oh my God, my hand is cold. Did you ever go to the circus? 0.1, 72.7, 0.1. Did you see the elephants? And the trapeze people? 0.1, 73.3.[13]

The rods make cranking sounds.

ROBIN: Yeah. 0.1. What was your favorite? Did you ever see the lions? 0.1, 0.2 … What was your favorite? How about the clowns? Did you ever see the clowns? 0.2, 72.5, 0.1, 0.2, 72.9. I always liked the elephants. I always liked it when the girl rode the elephants and made them dance. 0.1. It's 0 again, 73.1.

Indistinguishable whispering is heard.

ROBIN: 72.5, 0.1.

RENNE: (*Sensing something*) Hello.

ROBIN: So did you like the clowns? I always thought the clowns were kind of … worrisome. They were always a little …

A little girl giggling is distinctly heard.

ROBIN: Scary. 0.1.

GENE: Don't hit that glass (*referring to the rods*).

---

13. Even though it's not a significant decrease in temperature, you can see that it is steadily decreasing while the EMF is fluctuating, and first I and then Renne report feeling chills. Cold spots have often been theorized to be the result of an entity, whether consciously or unconsciously, drawing the energy out of the air. Humidity, vaporized water, holds latent energy. Hence, when the air becomes laden with moisture, rain starts falling and thunderstorms develop.

ROBIN: What was your favorite thing at the circus? Did you like the dogs? The last time I went to the circus they had dancing dogs. They would walk around on two legs, yeah, and dance around.

The rods crash into each other.

ROBIN: And they would jump through hoops. 72.1, 72.9, 73.4. We're back at a 0. (*To the spirit*) Make sure you talk in that box. You tell me, what was your favorite thing at the circus? (*To the group, referring to the spinning rods*) That's honestly not me. They don't usually react that way. (*To the spirit*) Are you still here? You see that box on the ground? You tell me, what was your favorite thing at the circus? We're at a 0, 73.4. Did your parents ever take you to the circus? With your brothers and sisters? (*Rod noises increase.*) Hmmm? You like to spin, don't you? You like that spinning.

RENNE: I feel like that thing is going to spin off and hit me.

ROBIN: (*To Renne*) They can't do that. (*To the spirit*) Did you ever have a top? They would spin, spin, spin, spin, spin. If you got them going really good, they would spin a long time. It's 0.0 now. Did you like spinning? Sometimes it felt like you were spinning out of control, didn't it? Sometimes life is kind of like that too. And now you're here in the hotel. Did you like to spin?

After hitting the ballroom, the Anna Suite, Room 16, and the hallway twice, our little band of investigators was tired. It was around midnight when we headed off to our rooms, Gene and I to the Anna Suite and Renne to Room 16. We left the audio and video recording.

With nine hours of video and audio footage collected that night, the material would take five investigators two months to review in total.

The Evidence

This is the report of the nine-minute exchange that we had in the second-floor hallway as presented to hotel personnel at the reveal.

2:18	Robin reports feeling chills.
3:32	Dowsing rods move so fast they hit a glass.
3:46	Rods spin uncontrollably.
4:11	Corresponding EMF fluctuations on Mel Meter: 0.1, 0.3, 0.2, 0.3, 0.2, 0.2, 0.2.
4:32	EMF fluctuations continue: 0.1, 0.2, 0.1. Temperature fluctuations: 72.2, 73.0, 72.9. Robin reports that her hand feels cold.
5:28	0.1, 73.3, 0.1, 0.2, 0.2, 72.5, 0.2, 72.9.
6:04	0.1, 72.0. EMF flatlines at 0.0. Then 72.2, 72.2, 72.5, 72.1.
6:30	Whispers.
6:34	Definite whispers.
6:40	Little giggle or whimper.

7:24 72.9, 73.4, and 0.0.

8:13 Rods spin wildly.

9:07 0.0.

9:36 Whisper.

During the second session on the second-floor hallway that night, I was asking the child a question, and there appeared to be a verbal response, although it isn't terribly clear what was said. Immediately after the voice, I again reported feeling chills. I really love it when evidence is layered in this manner. I'm not one to give a lot of credence to my own personal experiences. Every time I feel a chill or that tingly feeling in the back of my neck, I don't consider it evidence. But when I feel the physical sensation and it's backed up with other data or an EVP, I do feel far more comfortable considering it legitimate evidence.

Later during this same session, we got the true gem of the evening: an EVP of a child's voice answering a statement of mine. We heard a voice say, "No, it's not," as clearly as if a small child were standing next to me. It was so clear that the first time I heard it, I thought it was Renne. One of my team members had found the clip and sent it to me, and I was thoroughly confused. I thought, *What am I supposed to be hearing in this clip?* The second time I listened to it I nearly fell out of my chair—so clearly is it the voice of a child, in a hotel that doesn't allow children.

Second-Story Hallway

The child ghost may not be the only one to walk the second-story halls. During a time when the team was elsewhere and the hallway empty, we captured a strange recording of what sounded like an adult male, exhaling *ooooh aaaah*. A careful examination of the cameras showed the hallway to be empty at the time. I love evidence captured in empty spaces as free of contamination as a careful investigator can ensure.

Room 16

During the evening, when all three of us were out of the room, we recorded a long audio clip of what sounded like childish humming. The room was directly over the kitchen; however, we didn't pick up any other sounds of music coming from the kitchen. The only other room down this short hallway was Pat's, and she was away for the night. Eerily, the humming that was recorded went on and on intermittently for two or three minutes and then wasn't heard again the rest of the night. Raggedy Ann didn't receive any attention, unfortunately.

Anna Suite

Back in the Anna Suite, my husband and I were crawling into bed at the same time an EVP was recorded—a quick female voice instructed my husband to "rub her." We didn't hear the order at the time, and it was upon evidence review that I found the message. Then late, late in the night as my husband and I lay asleep, out of thin air a female voice with a thick southern accent directed my husband to "Jump up on her. Jump up on her." This remarkable voice was incredibly clear, captured amongst the sighs and rustlings of two people clearly asleep.

I often try not to read too much into the messages behind an EVP. In this case, however, the messages behind this disembodied voice seemed to support the notion of a female prostitute who still hadn't moved out of the Anna Suite. The fact that the EVPs appeared playfully sexual in nature supported the assertion. Best of all, she seemed to have liked me.

Unlike Matt, neither Gene nor I felt any feelings of uneasiness or dread in the room whatsoever. In fact, it seemed to me that the ghost in residence went out of her way to make sure I had a good time during my stay. Unfortunately, I was working that evening and didn't have any time for that type of nonsense, despite her best intentions.

Final Assessment

If anyone were to ask me formally if I thought the Atlantic Hotel was haunted, I would have to say yes. Despite contamination of the human kind that night, we got enough evidence for which there was simply no explanation: the voice recorder hidden in the bookshelf that produced a clear EVP of an adult female whispering clearly, "Can you hear me?"; the ghostly humming of a child in an otherwise empty Room 16; and the EVP of a female telling my husband to "jump up on her, jump up on her." All the evidence appeared to fit the legends surrounding the building.

I felt the activity in the Anna Suite might be residual—in other words, the actions of a prostitute long out of this world but still imprinted on the environment, such that the right stimulus caused a response. The child ghost on the second floor, however, was far too interactive with us, far too responsive to questions and conversations, to be classified as anything but intelligent. We also got three EVPs of what sounded distinctly like an adult female who also appeared interactive with us, demonstrating a certain intelligence as well.

The clearly male EVP we caught in an otherwise empty hallway would appear to suggest that the man who lost his life in the poker match gone bad might not have left entirely either. This might be simply residual energy, as no male entity interacted with us that evening. As we were unable to investigate Rooms 20 or 22, that question will probably remain unanswered until we return.

Postscript

Soon after we left, the hotel staff informed us that a couple was staying at the hotel one evening. Apparently, a knock on the door alerted them that someone was outside the room. According to the couple, the wife opened the door and found an older woman and a little girl standing outside. Her husband then approached the door and invited the woman and child into the room, at which point the apparitions appeared to dissolve before the couple's very eyes. The pair reported their extraordinary encounter to the front receptionist the very next morning in excited tones. It appeared they had seen two of the Atlantic Hotel's resident ghosts for themselves.

According to Matt, the couple appeared a little "out there." However, the evidence we collected seemed to support their claims. We distinctly heard an adult female whispering in several EVPs captured that evening. We also distinctly heard a child's voice humming, giggling, and answering our questions. It's certainly not out of the realm of possibility that the anonymous woman and the small child ghost might have formed some type of alliance.

CHAPTER 5
THE HAUNTED FORT ON THE BAY

Delaware City, Delaware

Fort Delaware on Pea Patch Island has become notorious for paranormal activity, mostly following the Atlantic Paranormal Society's (TAPS) two episodes on the hauntings at the fort and the filming of an episode of *Most Haunted.*

I actually had the opportunity to investigate the fort in 2008. It remains one of my most memorable paranormal investigations, even nearly a decade later.

Fort Delaware

An aging bastion of defense no longer viable to the military, the fort was abandoned after World War II and later acquired by the park service. It became a state park in 1951, open in the summers to school groups and interested tourists.

Straddled between the shores of Delaware and New Jersey, the island lies where the Delaware River becomes the bay. According to the legend, a ship carrying peas ran up against the mud, spilling out its load of peas. The peas took root and plants sprang up all over the muddy outcropping, creating the island. Whatever the true reason for the island, it is known that it is low and susceptible to the tidal marshes. For years after World War II, dredging operations dumped thousands of pounds of mud on the island. Thus, the island itself now sits a couple of feet higher than it did during the Civil War.

Fort Delaware.

Once you're inside the bricked walls of the fort, it's all about stepping back in time to the Civil War, which I'm not sure ever stopped being fought on that tiny spit of land. Reenactors in Civil War–era costume demonstrate daily what life was like at the time when the fort was actually a prisoner-of-war camp for Confederate soldiers. Women in homespun clothing demonstrate the old ways of baking bread on the open hearth, and a blacksmith demonstrates the basics of his trade, handing out handmade nails to school children. Soldiers in Union uniforms reenact how to fire a cannon or load a musket.

All this role-playing may be one of the reasons why the fort has the level of paranormal activity that visitors and employees encounter. The fort's heyday was during the Civil War, and thus reenactors mimicking that era would act to fuel the residual energy of the era.

The actual fort was built prior to the war, the bay being a defensible concern for the military. Pierre Charles L'Enfant, the French-born American military engineer who incidentally designed Washington, DC, first proposed building a bastion on the island in 1794. It wasn't until 1819, however, that military planners decided that the bay area needed a defensive installation and plans to build proceeded.

The first fort had structural issues and was mostly destroyed by fire in 1831. Plans for a new fort were delayed for ten years due to a legal battle over who owned the land. It was then–Secretary of War Jefferson Davis who helped approve an increase in the budget to build a pentagonal fort of brick to be built on six acres of land, with a moat surrounding it. This was ironic, as Davis would go on to become the commander in chief of the Confederate army and navy, and the fort would become a prisoner-of-war camp run by the Union.

Some twenty-five million bricks and large slabs of granite were transported to the island and set in place by a combination of hired workers and slave labor. They built what has been estimated as some of the finest brick arch masonry in the country, with graceful curved ceilings and portals. The semicircular metal cannon and gun mounts remain bolted to the floor to this day. The officers' quarters, by far the most elegant building on the compound, is a large red-brick building along the back wall of the fort. It had a large, sunny office space and its own kitchen on the first floor with bedrooms and sitting rooms for the officers and their families on the second floor. Noncommissioned officers (NCOs) didn't fare too badly either. They shared rooms on the third floor over what was the administration building.

Once completed, the fort was the best in the country. Manned as a protector of the shores and bay, a gun was never once fired from the fort in defense of the country. During the Spanish-American

War, it was used to protect the ports of Wilmington and Philadelphia and for munitions storage.

It was again sparsely manned during World War I as part of the coastal defense system. By the Second World War, it was determined that the aging fortress was obsolete and decommissioned. The island was abandoned, becoming simply a base for dredging operations in the bay and a curiosity spot for vandals and trespassers.

As already intimated, the fort's prime was during the Civil War, when it was used to imprison Confederate prisoners of war. The conversion of the fort's role from shore protection to POW camp occurred in 1862 with the arrival of 258 prisoners captured during the Battle of Kernstown. At its peak, the island prison held some 12,500 prisoners. In its four-year tenure as a POW camp, some 33,000 prisoners would pass through the fort, comprising not only Confederate soldiers but political prisoners and Union deserters.

The first prisoners were thus housed in the fort itself, in makeshift, poorly ventilated rooms that had been built to store munitions. These quickly overflowed with prisoners, at which point wooden sheds were erected on the parade ground, around which the walls of the fort were built. These quickly filled as well.

It became apparent to the military brass that the repurposing of the fort was more than a temporary measure. The Fort Delaware commander, Brigadier General Albin F. Schoepf, directed the building of squat wooden barracks along a large portion of the northwest side of the island, enough housing to intern 10,000 prisoners.

Crudely designed and built, the walls of these rectangular structures were lined with six-foot-wide wooden shelves three layers high, in which the men slept shoulder to shoulder, each building designed to hold up to 200 prisoners. Higher ranking prisoners were housed within the fort itself.

According to accounts, each prisoner was given one set of clothes, a "cheap" overcoat, and one blanket, inadequate protection against a wet, cold winter night. Within the drafty barracks was provided one or two small coal burning stoves—one or two stoves to provide heat for two hundred men. The damp marshy land, lack of clean drinking water, and inadequate protection against the ravages of winter led to widespread illness among the prisoners. Food also was in scarce supply. Scurvy, smallpox, dysentery, measles, and malnutrition ran rampant throughout the ranks. It's estimated that 2,460 prisoners died during their internment on Pea Patch Island.

Dr. W. H. Moon, Company 1, 13th Alabama Regiment, Archer's Brigade, wrote about his experience as prisoner: "Quite a number of the older men who required more food to sustain life became very much emaciated, and succumbed to the cold, being found on their bunks in the morning frozen to death. How any survived the ordeal through which we had to pass the winter seems strange to me now."[14]

Hundreds of the prisoners attempted escape, undaunted by the half-mile swim to shore. They tried to steal boats in some cases; others crafted crude rafts or attempted to float to shore on pieces of salvaged lumber or empty canteens. Perhaps the most desperate of the lot hid in privies and attempted to simply swim for it under the cover of nightfall. It is unknown how many men died attempting escape.

For several thousand prisoners, the only real escape from the island was in a crude pine box. Open boats took the dead from Pea Patch Island to the New Jersey shore. Those who died were buried at what is now Finn's Point National Cemetery. Sometimes six or seven boats a day would ferry the dead across to their final resting spot.

---

14. S. A. Cunningham, ed., *Confederate Veteran,* vol. 15 (Nashville, TN: S. A. Cunningham Proprietor, 1907), 213.

Following the end of the war, the final prisoners were released in 1866. By 1870, the fort was all but abandoned. Today, as one walks the long corridors of the fort, water drips from the walls and ceilings continually, limey stalactites grow from the tops of the curved ceilings, and hordes of bats make their home in niches in the walls. Graffiti from past prisoners is found etched in the walls. The water, the silence, and the call of distant seabirds remain as a lament to the suffering that was endured, a song to those who died on the island.

The State Park

The park itself opened in 1951 in an attempt to take the island back from the dredgers, vandals, and trespassers. As parks go, it was an expensive endeavor. The money required for the upkeep of such a compound, aging, sagging, and sinking into the marsh, forced park officials to find an alternative way to make money in order to keep the drawbridge open, as it were. It has always seemed to me that creating a revenue stream from publicizing the fort's paranormal activity was a less than desirable alternative for the park administrators. The local historians much preferred to talk about and demonstrate the history of the Civil War and the fort's contributions therein. However, the general public, as I've often bemoaned myself, would really just rather hear (or experience, in this case) a really good ghost story.

I was on board when the decision was made to open the park to ghost-hunting investigations every weekend in October. There is a lot of money to be made with tourism, if you have a taste for the macabre. The park director hoped to use the money made during the Halloween season for upkeep and repairs on the crumbling old fort. The park leaders realized that they'd found a gold mine. Now every weekend night in October, the ferry takes hundreds of tourists for a few hours of ghost hunting.

The Backstory

The paranormal activity of the fort is now that of urban legend. It has been written about in numerous books and recounted to large crowds of breathless spectators during ghost tours.

For one thing, numerous sightings of Civil War–era soldiers in gray uniforms have been reported by residents of nearby Delaware City. Wandering late at night down the near-deserted streets and alleyways, these apparitions appear to be searching for an escape route they never found. It is assumed that they are the apparitions of the weary souls who died during escape efforts and those who never made it home. Park employees have also witnessed soldiers. On dark, misty nights, apparitions of gray-clad Rebels have been spotted walking the reedy shoreline of Pea Patch Island, the fort's dungeons, and the desolately long, damp corridors of the fort.

Once the war was over and the fort was no longer used as a prison, the wood barracks structures were dismantled. Nothing of the prison barracks remained behind on the grassy plain that had held ten thousand prisoners. In 2001, park officials decided to give tourists a taste of what life had been like for the Rebel inmates. They used original plans to erect one barracks building that was an exact replica of the buildings that had once stood on the northern side of the island. That same year, reenactors of both armies spent a weekend on Pea Patch Island for their annual Garrison Weekend. Usually, the reenactors spent the weekend camping out in tents and sharing stories around campfires. That year, however, park officials decided to give the Confederate reenactors an accurate taste of what life as a POW on the island had been like: they put them up in the barracks.

The attendees arrived and stowed their gear in the building. They then went off to their day's events at the fort, the building locked and deserted by both reenactors and park officials. When the reenactors returned in the afternoon, they found that their gear had been rummaged through, their bags opened, and their clothes and possessions strewn around the building. Throughout the rest of the weekend, the attendees reported feelings of uneasiness in the structure. Some said they had heard odd tapping noises from the roof and under the floor. One reenactor swore he'd seen a canteen floating through the air. Built in the exact likeness of the structures of the era, it's not unlikely for the departed soldiers to have adopted the new structure as their residence.

Perhaps the most famous of the fort's ghost stories is the haunting of the sally port by Private Stefano. Just over the drawbridge is the main entrance to the fort, a rather majestic curved entryway called a sally port. Directly inside the structure and to the right is a set of stone stairs that lead up to the rooms of the second floor. During the Civil War, these rooms were used to house the Confederate officers. Private Stefano, an Italian immigrant, had apparently been assigned to the Rebel officers as an aide. Thus, he traveled around the fort during the day, running errands for his Confederate bosses. The stone stairs can be quite dangerous, the park rangers warned, especially during rainstorms or times of high humidity, as they become slick and slimy with mold. As legend has it, Stefano had been warned often to not run in the fort and to be especially careful of the sally port stairway, but he ignored the warnings. One fateful day, he was running down the slippery steps when he fell to his death upon the granite floor below. As for proving the story, there was a soldier named Stevens who fell to his death while working on the chapel, but that is the only actual related event that can be verified.

Now, as park rangers tell it, the sally port is haunted by the spirit of Private Stefano. During a ghost tour one night, a performer was retelling the story of Private Stefano to a group of fifty attendees when a young woman in the crowd became agitated. She stopped the story with a hysterical "He just touched me!" The historian stopped his recitation and asked the woman what she meant. She related that while standing in the crowd, she had seen a gray-uniformed soldier appear. And as he walked by her, the apparition had had the temerity to reach out and touch her arm. The woman was so frightened by what she had witnessed that she refused to continue the tour and left the building, electing instead to wait the two and a half hours for the ferry's return outside the walls of the fort.

Above the sally port are the rooms that were inhabited by the elite of the Confederate officers during the war. Today they are used as a place for park workers to don their Civil War costumes. Interviewed for a documentary entitled *Ghost Waters,* one of the park reenactors, Hank, recalled what had happened to him one morning in those very rooms. He said he had arrived early one morning for work and went up to a room above the sally port to dress in his costume. As he was finishing with his uniform, he looked up to see another uniformed man walk past the door of the room and down the hall. Hank stepped out into the hall, hoping to have a word with the man, as he would undoubtedly be working with him that day. Of course, Hank found that there was no one there. Except for a few doors to other such rooms, the hallway was a dead end. A quick perusal of the other rooms proved them empty. There was simply no man there and nowhere for him to have gone. Apparently, what

Hank had taken as a reenactor had instead been the real thing. Other reenactors have reported similar experiences.

Not all the spirits at the fort are soldiers, however. During a Halloween reading of Edgar Allan Poe's *The Raven* one evening, a crowd in the mess hall witnessed one of the lingering staff of the fort unwittingly. During the candlelit performance, the generator that provided power to the lights failed, plunging the room in near darkness. Daniel, the performer, quieted the crowd, demonstrating that they still had the one candle lit. He then finished his rendition of the poem. After the performance, the visitors took a tour of the fort and then departed the island.

A couple of weeks later, Daniel was approached by a couple who had been in the audience that evening. The woman commended Daniel on his reading and also said she had very much enjoyed the "cleaning lady" who had been part of the act. She said she knew the woman must have been a gag as he'd ignored her completely during the performance. A cunning bit of theatrics, the woman concluded.

Daniel was stymied. What could she possibly mean? What he got from the woman and her husband was that during the reading, a woman in period-style dress had come through a door in the wall to the right by the performer. She had approached the fireplace in the room and, using a feather duster, had dusted the mantel. Then she'd turned and gone back out of the room by the same door. They then told Daniel that their friends had also seen the mysterious woman. The four of them had talked about her after the show.

The story was made even odder when the facts of the architecture in that room were examined. The door from which the woman emerged was actually an exit that had been boarded up over the years. Behind the door is only about eight inches of door frame and then a solid wall. It's much too slender a space for a woman to have hidden in, awaiting her cue. Even more remarkable was the fact that the mantel the woman reportedly dusted was removed years ago. There is no mantel above the fireplace. The mantel-dusting phantom appeared to be a residual-style haunting. She has been seen several times by many people but always does the same thing: she comes through a door that no longer exists to dust a mantel that no longer hangs. What is extraordinary is how lifelike she appears to witnesses—so lifelike that the crowd during the show simply considered her a bit player.

In the officers' kitchen on the first floor of the brick building to the rear of the complex is a spirit who is more interactive. Described as a black woman in her thirties, she is said to stand around five foot six inches in height and bears a distinctive scar on her left cheek. She reportedly is witnessed wearing a blue cotton checkered dress with a white collar. Over the dress is a dirty white apron, singed at the bottom, probably from close exposure to the cooking fires over which she worked. The fort apparently employed many free African Americans during the war to work in the complex's kitchens and laundries. It is assumed she was a cook in the officer's kitchen and has never left her post.

Female reenactors at the fort often utilize the officers' kitchen in order to make period-appropriate food during tours. One such reenactor recalled a remarkable day while preparing food in the kitchen in 2005. Lauren, who was married to one of the fort's historians, recalled she was cooking in the kitchen with several children. They were cutting up vegetables at the large cook table in the center of the room, when Lauren looked over at the corner of the kitchen. Standing there motionless was the woman just described, watching her. Remarkably, the apparition remained for the better part of an hour, or so Lauren reported, during which time she moved about the room, looked into the pots, and nodded her head in approval of the food they were preparing. Lauren was fascinated. She recalled that she wanted very badly to speak with the apparition, but she was afraid to say anything in front of the children. Finally, the apparition appeared to walk through the wall in the same corner from where she had first emerged and disappeared.

The corner from which the ghost appeared has become somewhat notorious for being a cold spot. Investigators have reported as much as a 14-degree temperature drop at the spot. And one lucky visitor took a digital photograph of the corner and captured an image that appeared to be a shadowy outline of a woman in a dress with an apron.

Last among the infamous spirits of the fort is General Archer. In the long, dark, dank walkways of the munitions building a solitary man in a gray uniform and with a long beard has often been witnessed in his solitary walks. The apparition is thought to fit the description of the late General James Jay Archer.

Captured on the first day of the Battle of Gettysburg, Archer had been devising a plan to seize control of the fort with the help of his Confederate inmates. Unfortunately, one of Archer's confidants sold him out to General Schoepf, who ordered Archer to solitary confinement for three months and placed him on a diet of bread and water. Locked in a windowless, dank powder magazine, Archer emerged three months later a broken man. He died shortly thereafter. His apparition is always witnessed near the powder magazine in which he'd been held. When I tried to verify this story, I learned that Archer was only at the fort for a few weeks before he was transferred elsewhere. There is evidence he was planning to take over the fort, but there is no proof he was caught or confined in a magazine. He did die shortly after he was transferred from the fort.

The Investigation

The fort was rising in celebrity when my team was granted the opportunity of investigating. It had been investigated twice by TAPS. A few years before, the *Ghost Waters* episode had helped put it on the national map.

Still, the fort administrators hadn't yet fathomed selling tickets to would-be weekend warriors when my team approached the park director for permission to conduct an investigation. For a very expensive evening of ghost hunting (we had to pay the park and also take out special liability insurance lest one of us break a leg on Private Stefano's doomed staircase), I was able to investigate the fort with only eleven other individuals. Twelve people and a small handful of park rangers to investigate a fort of this size was manna from heaven. As long as everyone played by the rules, there was very little threat of contamination. We were assigned to teams, and I spent most of the evening with Tammy and Mary, who was actually a member of a different group. At times we were accompanied by a park ranger, and at other times we were on our own. The quiet, dark fortress hallways, the parade ground where dark shadows were seen moving about, the kitchen where the female apparition had been seen stirring something in an empty pot, the empty NCO barracks where the general public was not admitted (even the officers' quarters usually glassed off with partitions were all opened for us that evening)—the world was truly our paranormal oyster, and we were there to pluck the pearl should we find it.

I started the evening walking the damp hallways of the fort surrounds. Pitch dark and dripping water, there really wasn't a lot we experienced, but I did have an interesting dowsing rod experience. Walking around with my rods, I found an area under one of the archways where the rods seemed to be spinning much more vigorously. I asked a team member to come over with an EMF detector in the same spot, and it demonstrated an EMF spike. This is a part of the building with no electricity. It was a clarifying experience.

After an hour, we regrouped. My team was assigned a park ranger and sent off to the NCO barracks. It was then that the night became much more interesting. In an area of the fort that the general public never gets to visit, the NCO barracks were a number of smallish rooms off a central corridor. Mostly used now for storage, the small rooms held paint cans and stacks of wood.

Throughout our time in the area, we heard a number of odd sounds, always seeming to come from the other end of the hall from where we were situated.

We wandered from room to room for a while, finally settling in one room about midway down the hall. It should be said that a short but very virulent thunderstorm had rolled over the small island just previously. Thus, we were told by park officials that we were to stay put until further notice. We found it to be no hardship whatsoever. The conversation we had up in the NCO barracks was one of the most exciting exchanges I've ever experienced in ten-plus years of investigating.

We situated our equipment about the room for the exchange. We had two video cameras (one malfunctioned), audio recorders, EMF detectors, and temperature gauges. Tammy pulled out a pair of dowsing rods and appeared to have a long conversation with someone unseen.

We were employing the technique in which the rods indicated a yes response when crossed. When uncrossed, the rods signified either a no or neutral response. After every yes response, or crossing of the rods, we asked the rods to return to a neutral position of uncrossed, which they did upon request.

The entity with whom we appeared to be communicating actually indicated that he was not from the Civil War era when the fort was so actively in use, but from a later time, perhaps around the First World War, when, as my research indicated, the fort was still in use. He confirmed that he had been stationed on the island at the time. He had fallen in love with an officer's wife, but the love was unrequited and at some point he had taken his own life. Whether this rather tragic, rather convenient story was true, I've never been able to ascertain. However, during the exchange, an EMF detector placed on the floor by Tammy's feet began reacting to the questions as well. Tammy's video recorder, placed on the bunk bed in the room, malfunctioned. It had been recording without incident all night but stopped inexplicably during the exchange. Thankfully, my beloved Panasonic DVC camera with the IR setting recorded without incident.

Tammy was working the rods during the session, and we placed an EMF detector at her feet. The rest of the equipment was scattered about the room in what we hoped would be strategic locations. Through yes and no answers, we had ascertained that the spirit we were talking to was a corporal, a lower-ranking enlisted man. He had indicated that he had fallen in love with a woman, possibly the wife of an officer, and that the relationship had ended badly. Someone unfamiliar with military rank may not fully comprehend the disparity between officers and enlisted members of the military. Honestly, it always struck me as the last holdover of feudal society remaining in our country. The hierarchy is clear. Officers are considered the elite aristocracy of the military. They are afforded the best housing and food—and treatment, for that matter. The enlisted are the common workers, the lowest rankings being the working force, the higher enlisted acting more as middle management. The officers make the decisions, the enlisted men make it happen. So, for a corporal to mingle with an officer's wife is an unthinkable breach of etiquette, a situation not likely to end well for the enlisted man.

The rods had crossed at *E* when we asked what the first initial of his name had been. I'd been racking my brain for any name that started with an *E* afterward, but the rods gave a no to every name I suggested. I then asked if we could give him a pseudonym by which to address him, but he wouldn't have it.

Here is a transcript of the recorded events, *in medias res*:

TAMMY: So the woman, she was the wife of an officer stationed at Fort Mott? (*The dowsing rods cross.*) Yes.

ROBIN: Yes. What were you doing, Corporal, with an officer's wife? Okay, okay, okay. I don't…

The rods move erratically.

PARK RANGER: KII hit. KII hit (*referring to the EMF detector at Tammy's feet*).

ROBIN: Big time?

PARK RANGER: Big time when you were talking about that.

MARY: There he goes.

PARK RANGER: [The EMF detector]'s going.

ROBIN: Is it? Damn it, I wish I had [my camera] up.

MARY: Did her husband find out about it?

ROBIN: It is 67 degrees by Tammy. It is 77 degrees on the floor.

TAMMY: Uncross the rods, please. Calm down, calm down. We're not trying to upset you.

The rods rock erratically.

ROBIN: Don't get upset. We're not trying to upset you.

PARK RANGER: We're not going to question why you did this.

ROBIN: I know you said that your name started with an *E*, how about we call you Ed? Would Ed be okay? (*The rods separate further.*) No, huh, you don't like Ed?

TAMMY: What other names start with *E*? Does your name start with *E*? (*The rods distinctly cross immediately.*) Uncross, uncross the rods, please.

ROBIN: Okay, well, I guess we'll just call you Corporal then. Is that okay? (*The rods cross.*) Corporal? Corporal, listen up. (*The rods cross.*) You do know that people make all sorts of silly mistakes in their lives, don't you? (*The rods move apart.*) Sometimes they really, really hurt. Do you understand that? There you go. (*The rods immediately and emphatically cross.*)

PARK RANGER: Two big ones [KII hits].

ROBIN: I myself have made some very bad mistakes in my life. Uncross those, sweetheart.

PARK RANGER: There's big time. There's big time [spikes] to your questions.

TAMMY: Robin, I'm taping on mine so go ahead and [shoot video at the floor at the EMF meter].[15]

ROBIN: All right. Corporal, so my question is to you. You make that KII go off if you understand me…

The EMF detector lights up at her request.

PARK RANGER: The light on the floor.

The EMF meter goes off again.

ROBIN: Yeah. Do you think that you could…? (*The KII meter goes off in response*). Okay, thank you. Do you think you could find it in your heart to forgive yourself? (*KII meter goes off several times.*) Can you forgive yourself for what you have done?

MARY: I think that's a no.

PARK RANGER: It's okay, Corporal. (*The KII still continually lights up.*) You can forgive yourself.

Lights on EMF meter are solid at this point.

ROBIN: Corporal, would you like us to pray for you? Yes?

The team performs a short prayer for the Corporal and then continues.

ROBIN: Does that feel better? Good. Now God can forgive you for this. Can you forgive you for this?

The EMF detector flashes in the low ranges almost continually.

ROBIN: Corporal, go home, honey, and find your people. And forgive yourself for this, okay? You don't have to stay here any longer. (*The EMF detector returns to 0.*) Will you do that for us?

---

15. Tammy had her video recorder set up and recording on the top bunk of the room. We would later realize that it had shut down without explanation during the entire exchange.

I'm not sure what the ranger's feelings about the fort's paranormal activity were before that evening, but by the end of this session, he was an active and enthusiastic participant in the exchange. I believe he was rather moved by the whole event, being former military himself.

Directly after the remarkable session in the NCO barracks, our small team moved to the officers' kitchen, where the female cook was reported to reside. The three of us were in the kitchen with the door open to the courtyard. We were conducting a question-and-answer session using the dowsing rods. We had EMF detectors and voice recorders going as well. I recorded the whole session on my video recorder for posterity. We used the rods to answer yes/no questions, crossed for yes and uncrossed for no or neutral, as we had in the NCO barracks.

TAMMY: (*Holding the rods*) Okay, does anyone want to ask any questions?

ROBIN: Can we talk to the person who used to be the cook here? No? Is she not present?

Distinct sound of a footstep or shuffling echoes from out in the courtyard. Tammy stops and turns her head, looking back toward the door.

ROBIN: Is she not present? We want to talk to the cook.

Tammy hears the shuffling again and looks confused. She holds up a hand to pause the session. They all wonder why there was movement in the courtyard, as all teams were supposed to be in their locations and not moving about, in order to control contamination.

TAMMY: Wait. Wait a minute (*listening*).

MARY: I thought I just heard footsteps out there.

TAMMY: That's what I [thought]. And I can't tell if it's raining, but I heard, I heard two perfect, two different, very distinct…

MARY: I heard footsteps.

TAMMY: It's not the rain; it's footsteps out there. I mean it's raining too, but...

Mary and Tammy walk over to the kitchen door and look out into the courtyard. There is a small sound on the audio that might be an owl.[16]

ROBIN: Is someone out there?

MARY: Now I don't hear it.

TAMMY: No, I heard footsteps. I heard two.

Robin retrieves one of the EMF detectors and heads into the courtyard area, followed by Mary.

ROBIN: Is someone out here? Is someone out here?

A park ranger comes out of another building when he hears the team talking in the courtyard.

ROBIN: No, we just heard walking. (*To the spirit*) If you're out here, can you walk up to the green light? It will flash and tell us that you're here.

There is a long pause.

ROBIN: Can you make something move? Can you move something? Can you give us a sign of your presence?

TAMMY: (*Still in the kitchen, astonished*) Did somebody just say "no"?

ROBIN: No.

---

16. The park rangers confirmed there was at least one owl that called the fort home.

MARY: Neither of us.

TAMMY: I just literally heard someone say (*whispering loudly*) "nooo." And it sounded like it was coming from right outside the door.[17]

Robin returns to the kitchen.

ROBIN: (*To Tammy*) Okay. (*Turns around and goes back out.*) Are you still here? Is someone trying to communicate with us?

A couple of minutes later, Robin and Mary return to the kitchen.

TAMMY: I really thought it was you.

ROBIN: I almost thought I heard whispering (*points out the door*). But this rain—it's hard to … I mean, I wouldn't swear to it in a court of law, but I almost thought I heard whispering over at the cannon. And then …

TAMMY: Well, that walk was very distinct. Hopefully one of the recorders picked it up.

ROBIN: Okay, we're back in the kitchen.

TAMMY: All right, I'm going to put my voice recorder out in the hallway because I'm hearing stuff tonight.

ROBIN: All right, well, we don't need three in here, so …[18]

TAMMY: (*Holding rods*) Did you work in the kitchen so you didn't have to fight? Could you not fight and that's why you had to work in the kitchen? Aha, uncross please.

MARY: Are you hearing voices out there?

---

17. There is no audible whispered "no" on the recording, except for Tammy's.

18. In the audio recording, I later detected sounds at this point that sounded like very low whispering three times. We didn't hear them at the time.

Robin: Someone is out there.

Tammy: Yes, there's someone out there. There's flashlights. I just saw flashes of light.

Robin: Mmhm.

Tammy: Were you injured? Uncross please. Were you injured in battle? Uncross please. Were you injured in Gettysburg? Okay. (*Rods cross.*) Uncross please.

The low sound of voices echoes out in the courtyard.

Tammy: There's somebody out there.

Robin: That one was unmistakable (*laughs*).

Tammy: Okay, were you injured at Gettysburg? Now we're going to get a no. Rods uncross. I feel like I'm playing Jeopardy. Uncross please.

Mary: Was it an accident?

Tammy: All right, uncross. (*Rods move erratically.*) Calm down.

Robin: Did you fight for the South? (*Small, unidentifiable high-pitched sound.*) Did you fight for the North?

Tammy: All right, uncross please. Your injury was an accident? (*Rods cross.*) Were you injured in a battle in the North? Were you injured in a battle in the South?

Suddenly, there is a gargantuan banging sound like the sound of a cannon being fired. The sound reverberates all over the fort but is loudest in the kitchen, so loud and so immediate that the three investigators are overwhelmed in a sheer unconscious panic. They are so startled they flee the table where they had gathered and run to the other side of the room simultaneously, while yelling at the top of their lungs. They huddle together like cattle in a snowstorm. Tammy's dowsing rods are now in Mary's hands. Robin clutches her beloved Panasonic that had been mounted on a tripod.

Gasps and shushing sounds are heard as they try to reclaim rational thought.

TAMMY: Okay, okay.

MARY: Why am *I* holding the rods?

All three explode in laughter.

It is extremely interesting to point out that the first time the TAPS team investigated the fort in June 2008, Jason Haws and Grant Wilson were investigating in the same kitchen and experienced much the same bang as the three of us experienced that night. Jason actually dropped the rolling pin he was holding at the time, the sound being so astonishingly loud. During our investigation, there was a reporter from the *Delaware State News* on hand. In her article about the investigation, Ali Cheeseman quoted one of the park rangers on hand as saying that the sound was distinctly like that of a friction primer used to fire cannons.

And about the frequent sounds of footsteps and dark figures we had seen in the courtyard… After the explosive bang occurred, everyone in the fort was questioned about where they had been and whether they had been wandering the courtyard. We explained that we had seen dark figures and even what we took to be a flashlight. No one admitted to having been wandering the courtyard. They all stated that they had been in their designated areas as directed.

Still, not everyone on my heroic team was convinced that we had seen shadowy figures and heard the sound of a ghostly cannon. Some of our more skeptical members examined doors to see if any had inadvertently slammed shut. None were found closed. Team members Dom and Collin returned to the fort another day to examine the sounds of a friction primer and a musket being fired in order to rule out possibilities.

The Evidence

The following is an excerpt from the evidence log for the NCO barracks encounter session, which began at 11:20 p.m. with Robin, Tammy, Mary, and the park ranger.

26:19	Dowsing rods crossed while Tammy moves to the corner. Tammy reports that something is disturbing them. They're swinging erratically.
27:10	Rods move back to neutral. Group is asking for "it" to come out of corner and speak with them.
28:18	Corporal from Pennsylvania: no for Pittsburgh, PA.
28:44	"Really high EMF meter spike."
29:08	Rods crossed affirmative for Pennsylvania again; crossed for Philadelphia.

29:38 Rods crossed yes for corporal.*

30:36 Rods crossed yes when asked if the corporal had died here.

30:55 Rods acting erratic.

31:26 Spirit confirmed he was not from Germany (not a WWII POW) but Pennsylvania. Confirmed he died in 1944.

31:55 Three EMF spikes in quick succession at meter by Tammy's feet.

32:24 Rods cross yes for army. He'd been a corporal in the army.

32:42 Rods confirm that an accident by gunshot had caused the corporal's death.

33:24 Rods separate in a no for gunshot inflicted by another person.

33:37 Rods confirm that the spirit had shot himself.

* It's good practice to re-ask questions to see if you get the same response, thereby building the credibility of the experience.

33:37	"Did you hurt yourself?" Rods cross yes then start to act erratically—the team tries to calm the spirit down.
34:04	Tammy reports feeling very cold.
34:40	"Would you like to go home?" Rods confirm yes.
34:53	Tammy again reports feeling very cold. Temperature reading on the floor in the center of the room indicates 79 degrees Fahrenheit, with 73 degrees air temperature.
35:46	Tammy reports that the entity has "backed off."
36:08	Rods cross yes to confirm that the corporal had actually been stationed at Fort Mott, not Fort Delaware.
36:17	Rods cross when they ask if he'd "hurt himself" over a woman.
36:32	Tammy again reports feeling cold.
36:59	Temperature by Tammy is 71 degrees (an 8-degree difference from the center of the room).

37:26 Rods cross to confirm that the woman had been married to someone else.

37:45 Rods cross to confirm that the woman in question knew that the corporal had cared for her.

38:36 Rods cross when they ask if he knew that the woman was very likely dead now. Temperature readings around Tammy indicate the temperature was decreasing: 70, 69, 68.

41:31 Mary reports a noise when they ask the spirit about suicide. Park ranger confirms that Fort Mott was still a working fort during WWII but that Fort Delaware had been decommissioned.

42:15 Rods cross when they ask if he'd "snuck" onto the island, as during this time period the fort would have been abandoned.

43:00 Rods cross when they ask if he had planned to rendezvous with someone on the island.

46:00 Rods crossed to confirm that he came to meet the woman here. She didn't show, and so he "hurt" himself.

47:36	Rods crossed to confirm that the woman had been the wife of an officer at Fort Mott.
47:40	EMF spikes reported. Rods acting erratically. 67 degrees by Tammy; 77 degrees on the floor.
48:00	Rods crossed yes to confirm that his name started with an *E*. Rods were neutral when they ask if his name was Earl or Ed. Team tries several *E* names, but the rods never confirm a yes. Finally, they ask if it would be okay to call him "Corporal." The rods cross yes.
49:25	"Big time spikes" on EMF detector reported by park ranger.
49:44	Two more EMF spikes.
50:04	Rods crossed yes when they ask if he would like them to pray for him.
51:22	EMF spike.

Unfortunately, we gathered no video evidence of apparitions that evening. There were no stationary cameras trained on the parade ground or courtyard areas, or we might have recorded some of the dark shapes we three witnessed while in the kitchen. We also failed to capture video evidence at Private Stefano's steps. One team, however, recorded an odd sound in the sally port area for which they could not account. The mantel dusting apparition in the mess hall was not caught on tape.

At the reveal, Seth, a park employee, and fellow team members Collin and Dom recalled an incident that happened directly after the bang in the kitchen, an incident of which I had been unaware. Apparently, those investigators and park employees who were in the near vicinity came quickly when they heard the bang and then the screams. Dom, Collin, and Seth admitted that as they approached the kitchen and laundry area, they distinctly heard the sound of footsteps on the wooden floor overhead. As all the team members had been accounted for, they assumed that a trespasser had somehow snuck into the fort. The third-floor parapet section was connected by two staircases. They chose different staircases and vowed to meet in the middle, hoping to catch the trespasser somewhere in between. However, once on the third floor, they found no one. They admitted they were rather stunned, as the footsteps had been so distinct.

Seth described the experience on camera: "A few seconds after that [bang], we thought we heard distinct footsteps overhead. You know where the library is? We heard—" Seth thumps with his hands on the wood table to demonstrate the sound they clearly heard. "We knew there was someone up there. But at that point we didn't know who it could be, as everyone was accounted for ... They came back in after hearing [the bang], and then we heard the thumping, and we thought, *Okay, that was a little weird.* That was when we went to the two ends [of the second-floor battlement]. The only way to come down is the side on the third tier and the other side where there's the spiral staircase. And we got nothing. No one came out of the laundry area. We found nothing. We don't know where they went."

Collin heard the bang and then the discernible footsteps. He raced with the others to the top of the battlements but found no one. Fearing someone was meddling with the investigation, he pointedly asked the park employees whether they were indeed the only ones on the island. He defended his questioning about whether the fort had been breached by saying, "We thought someone was in the fort. After that happened, I had to grab Seth. I had to ask that question."

An audio recorder in the kitchen recorded the sound of footsteps. When played at the reveal, they were quite audible and very distinct. Also, at the reveal Dom noted a further parallel to the TAPS investigations of the fort: "If you take notice of the live show, every group that was in that kitchen thought there was someone on the stairwell that we went up. Now we chased something that night. We thought someone was in the fort. We went up both sides, and there was no one there."

Dom further noted that his team had been in the NCO barracks leading up to the bang, the same barracks where my team had had the interesting dowsing rods and EMF exchange earlier in the night. Dom noted that just prior to the bang, his team had also distinctly heard footsteps up there.

Also collected that evening were a handful of interesting EVPs. Both Dom and I caught EVPs of a male voice that seemed to say "hello" during our time in the Endicott section of the fort.

Collin's team heard a disembodied voice in the area of the officers' kitchen and laundry area. On the recording, you hear what sounds like a female voice saying something briefly, and then a team member responds by asking the question, "What was that?" What the female voice said was actually indistinguishable.

In the kitchen, another team also caught an EVP, which appeared to also be female and sounded very much like the female voice in the laundry room. This EVP clearly said, "I'm here."

They also recorded an odd sound of whistling in the courtyard just outside the kitchen and laundry room area. They didn't hear the sound at the time. On the EVP, it distinctly sounded like someone whistling off tune.

Interestingly, all the EVPs were captured either in the Endicott section of the fort or in the area right around the officers' kitchen, laundry, and courtyard area, where the distinct footsteps and the big bang occurred as well.

Final Assessment

The sound of the cannon firing was probably the most profound event of the evening. I feel the fact that the TAPS crew had a similar experience indicates that this is a residual type of sound. Residual activity acts in this way. When the environmental factors are correct, when the temperature, or possibly the humidity, is just right, these phenomena occur regardless of who may be lucky enough to be recording at the time. The fact that this particular phenomenon has been captured twice makes it an extraordinarily valuable piece of evidence.

Many of Fort Delaware's spirits undoubtedly fall under the residual haunting category. Not really a haunting at all, this is an imprint of people long past, replaying when the conditions are correct. My best guess is that the footsteps in the courtyard and parade ground, the dark shapes we spotted several times during our interlude in the kitchen, and the footsteps Dom's team heard in the NCO barracks all fall into the residual category.

If water is a component of residual hauntings, as many experts in the paranormal field believe, then Fort Delaware is a prime location for residual style activity, as it's surrounded by a feudal-style moat of water and situated on an island. It's not out of the realm of possibility that some of the events of the past left an imprint on the fort and the surrounding areas as well.

Any evidence of an intelligent haunting, such as EVPs or disembodied voices, seemed to center around the kitchen, laundry room, and courtyard area of the fort. This is where staff had reported witnessing a female apparition and a consistent cold spot and also where the team caught most of the EVPs that evening. In other words, our findings seemed to be consistent with the previous reports. It's certainly not inconsistent for a complex of this size and history to have a combination of intelligent and residual activity.

Postscript

Years later, I needed some photographs of the fort for my first book, so I decided to pay the price of admission and return to the fort for a night of ghost hunting with around fifty of my best friends... In other words, I agreed to do the tourist thing for the night in order to get a few good pics. Honestly, with that many people, I seriously doubted I'd experience anything except wet shoes and a chilly sea wind. We were sent in groups of about ten people, including two or more chaperones from the paranormal group that hosts the tours. They were very gracious hosts, I must admit. They offered to let us use their equipment and even lent me a pair of dowsing rods.

In the laundry room I was lucky enough to have a dowsing rod conversation with a spirit who claimed to be an unmarried woman who had worked at the fort. To a rapt audience, the rods confirmed that the woman with whom I was conversing was an older woman who had labored as a laundress during the Civil War. She'd never had children, she professed. Unfortunately, although the room was peppered with EMF gauges and audio recorders, we got no hits on the meters nor messages on the recorders—at least not on our *audio* recorders. So while the rod conversation wouldn't be admissible evidence, it was another truly interesting exchange. And it could be noted that this is the area that our team felt had the highest indication of an intelligent-style haunting.

While we were in the area of the building where they had once stored munitions and sold uniforms, known as the Endicott section, we thought we might be hearing the sound of footsteps overhead. Unfortunately, we couldn't be sure, and then one overenthusiastic attendee ran over with a squawking ghost box, making it impossible to hear anything at all.

Of course, even if we had heard footsteps, who is to say that someone wasn't walking around on the second floor with another group? Contamination, my old friend. This is why I don't attempt to do paranormal research with fifty other people present.

While we were in the same area, I wandered away from the group and stood gazing into the munitions storage room. Quiet observation is one of the best skills an investigator can learn. It's usually when you least expect it, and are not demanding it, that paranormal activity occurs. As I stood there by myself gazing into the dark, deserted room, I thought I saw a dark shadowy figure emerge from the other shadows and very briefly move from left to right. It was a very short encounter, and I couldn't be sure of what I'd seen. As I continued to stare, perhaps half a minute later a park ranger walked up to the window and entered the building. I surmised that the moving shadow had been cast by him as he moved across the parade ground and up to the building.

I did have a video camera trained on the room and recording. I vowed that I'd carefully examine the video the next day. Upon analysis, I sadly found that the camera's angle was slightly different than mine had been. I saw no moving black shadow.

So, while I came away with no evidence on this trip, I did get a couple of really nice pictures and a good story nearly a decade later.

PART II

ACCOUNTS COLLECTED

CHAPTER 6
MATT'S HOUSE

Berlin, Maryland

After Matt, the maintenance manager of the Atlantic Hotel in Berlin, Maryland, gave us the tour of the building, we stood in the parking lot talking. He said that while the hotel had a haunted reputation, its activity was nothing compared to what he had experienced in his own home. I kept the recorder going as Matt launched into the chilling details. Immediately, he made it clear that while he would talk to us about the property, he wouldn't let us investigate the home. He feared that bringing in a team would cause the activity to increase at a time when it was relatively quiet. Many people, I've found, take this view; they fear that having a band of strangers in to investigate a property would only anger the spirits, thereby inciting more activity. Besides, Matt and his wife, Noelle, had had the property investigated once before, and what the team uncovered convinced them not to do it again.

I don't push the matter with people because I cannot guarantee that after an investigation their situation will be better, and I don't want to be the one responsible for making their lives more unbearable. While it's fun to read about a haunted house or watch it on TV, it's another matter to live in a home where paranormal activity occurs. The threat of the unknown, the feeling that you're never alone, the hair-raising sensation of being watched during your most private moments—all these factors are very unsettling.

Many of the historic buildings in Berlin are reportedly haunted. The town being old and with the closeness of water, the chances of paranormal activity increases. However, Matt's home, as he would later find out, had earned a reputation with the local townspeople for being haunted.

The house that Matt lived in was built sometime in the 1930s. The original owner was a woman named Mary who lived in the home until she was in her eighties. It's unknown whether she died in the structure. Matt's parents eventually purchased the property as an investment property sometime between 1996 and 1997 from a man named Dwayne, who had used the barn behind the house as a motorcycle repair shop. The property also had the original house and a mother-in-law suite behind the main house, where Dwayne had resided for several years.

Matt's father had intended to use the barn for a business of some type and live on the second floor, but the barn first needed major renovations. Matt's parents took up residence in the main house for six months while construction commenced on the barn. Matt said neither of his parents ever reported feeling anything strange in the house while they lived in it. Matt admitted that his father was an avowed nonbeliever in the paranormal, and his mother was simply unaware of her surroundings most of the time. The renovations completed, Matt's parents moved out of the house and into the barn, at which time they started renting out the front of the house.

At the time, none of it made much difference to Matt, who actually lived and worked in Florida. He moved back to the area eventually, and he and his first wife, Carrie, lived in the Baltimore-Glen Burnie area of Maryland. They used the mother-in-law suite on weekend getaways to the shore. He noted that his first indication that there might be something amiss with the house was when he and Carrie were having a yard sale one weekend day. The renovation of the property had left, apparently, a good number of items that Matt's parents wanted to be rid of, and so Matt and Carrie were manning the yard sale. An elderly woman stopped by to look at the items on display. She asked about something in particular, and Carrie said that she had one, but it was in the house. She invited the woman in to see it. And that's when the exchange became odd.

According to Matt, the older woman said quite adamantly, "Oh no, I won't go in that house. I know all about it."

Confused about what the woman was alluding to, Carrie asked, "What do you mean?"

The woman responded, "I know all about that house. It's the ghost house."

As with many houses with a dark reputation, it appeared that the neighbors knew all about the house's past. Since that sale, Matt said he'd had several neighbors tell him about the house's haunted reputation.

Matt recalled that early on while visiting the house, he really didn't experience much in the way of the paranormal. Mostly, it was benign things that Matt simply chalked up to a poor memory. His keys would go missing, small items would get moved. One time he lost his MP3 player. He looked high and low for the it, as he had all his music on it. Eventually, he gave it up for lost. Months later, he went to the kitchen to make a pot of coffee, as he did every day. Carrie didn't drink coffee, so he was the only one in the house who ever touched the coffee supplies. There in the nest of his coffee filters, inexplicably, was his MP3 player. What was even odder, according to Matt, was the fact that while it had been missing for the better part of three months, the device was still fully charged. The episode left Matt thoroughly confused, but he still didn't consider the experiences paranormal.

Then one evening, he and Carrie came face-to-face with the fact that the property might have unseen inhabitants. Matt and Carrie were having a heated argument over "something stupid," according to Matt. In a pique of irritation, Matt finally gave up the fight and announced he had had enough and was going to bed. Lying quietly in bed, he became frozen in fear. He distinctly heard the sound of footsteps thumping around in the attic overhead. Why, Matt wondered, would someone be up in their attic? According to Matt, the attic to the building is only accessible from the mother-in-law suite where he and Carrie resided when they came. The tenants to the front of the building had no access to the attic from their apartment. Thus, it couldn't be the tenant in the front apartment—and yet Matt distinctly heard the sound of angry-sounding footfalls stomping around. Carrie apparently hadn't heard the sounds. She was still arguing her point when Matt told her to be quiet and listen.

Sensing something was wrong, Carrie stopped talking, and both listened to the sounds of footfalls eventually leaving the attic and coming down the stairs. Finally, the footfalls stopped at their bedroom door. And then Matt noticed something else, something even more chilling. Despite the fact that it was August and very warm, both Matt and Carrie could see their breath in the sudden chill. "The windows were open, and it was a really warm evening, and yet suddenly we were freezing. The argument was immediately over." Carrie dove into bed next to Matt, and both lay waiting for what might be coming in the bedroom door at them, but nothing did. Eventually, the sound of footfalls died away, and Matt noted that the oppressive feeling withdrew. It was as if something or someone had had enough of listening to the couple's bickering and decided to make it stop.

Eventually, Matt and Carrie went their separate ways. After the split, as is often the case with divorces, Matt found himself in a bit of a financial bind. So while he had never intended to, he moved permanently to his parent's rental house and became a full-time resident of the mother-in-law suite. The front apartment of the house still had renters. Between Matt's first wife and his second, he lived alone in the back apartment with his two large dogs for five years. He admitted that aside from things going missing and the oppressive air of the place, things were fairly quiet in the house. He did note that girlfriends he dated throughout the five years were often uncomfortable in the apartment.

Matt recalled one event during that five-year span with vivid recollection. He estimated that it happened around the year 2000.

It started as a mundane morning. Alone in the apartment except for the two dogs, Matt was in his bathroom taking a shower. The shower stall had a glass door, through which he could view the room. He'd had his back to the door, and then, he said, "I turned around, and through the glass shower door, I could clearly see someone standing there, in my bathroom." Matt described the figure as being relatively short, only around five feet tall. Still, considering that Matt was in the shower and completely defenseless while a stranger was standing in his bathroom, it was terrifying. "It was definitely a person. And I'm like, 'Oh my God, I'm so vulnerable right now.'"

He turned back to turn the water off, and when he turned back around, there was no one in the room. Yet Matt knew he'd seen a figure standing in his bathroom moments ago, and if the person had been in the bathroom, he'd now be in the apartment. Matt stood still for a moment, not knowing what to do. Needing some way to defend himself, he devised a quick plan. He thrust the door to the shower open, jumped out, quickly grabbed a towel to wrap around himself, and then scooped up the tank cover from the toilet, it being the heaviest item that came to hand. Armed with a weapon, he left the bathroom and searched the rest of the apartment, only to find no one. No one was in the apartment, there were no signs of forced entry, and the dogs showed no sign of distress. Matt continued, "I thought, *Oh my God, what did I just see?* That freaked me out. I mean, the figure I saw wasn't very tall—it was short. But what I saw was a figure. I couldn't really see any details through the glass, but I saw a figure. I saw what I saw. That event scared me. I mean, that one was legit. I saw something, and it was bad."

Still, Matt said that after the event, nothing really happened in the apartment for a while. He admitted that he continued to lose items or to find items in odd locations. He'd wonder, *I had a couple of beers last night. Did I just forget where I put things?* "But that could just have been me. It was stupid stuff." Thus, Matt brushed most of the odd occurrences off as lapses in memory. Time went by and nothing of note happened.

Eventually, Matt reconnected with Noelle. They'd dated when she had been in middle school and Matt in high school. Matt had given her rides to school. There'd been an attraction even then, but Matt, realizing he was too old for her, had told Noelle that he couldn't date her then but that at some time in the future they'd be together. Apparently, in a storybook ending, that time was now. They met and reconnected, and Noelle and her daughter, Alexa, moved in with him.

At the time, Alexa was quite small, only around three, according to Matt. Still, Alexa came to Matt with a chilling story. One day she told Matt about seeing a woman in her room, an older woman. "She was little at the time, and so I didn't really press her," Matt said, but admitted that her account worried him.

Then Alexa said she'd seen a gray mist. She'd been asleep on the sleeper sofa in the living room. When she woke, she'd spotted a coalescing gray mist that appeared to be advancing toward her. She screamed and the mist dissolved. Again, Matt didn't press for too many details. Since she was so young, he didn't want to frighten the little girl any more than he had to.

However, after these events, Matt would stay up late at night, long after Noelle and Alexa went to bed, just to make sure they were safe. Nothing else happened to make Matt worried.

Realizing that his growing family needed more room, the front tenants were sent packing. Matt then quickly renovated the front apartment, getting the renovation and repainting done in a matter of weeks. The new family then moved to the front apartment, and the rear went up for rent.

The new apartment was fine, according to Matt, until he decided to tip the apple cart and actually ask Noelle to marry him. Already an employee at the Atlantic Hotel, he decided to make the event memorable by proposing to his high school sweetheart at the historic hotel. Alexa spent the day with her grandmother, who incidentally is DPRG's co-director, Renne.

Matt said he'd been a bachelor for a while, so he'd decorated his apartment in like fashion. He'd bolted a lacrosse stick to the living room wall in addition to a skateboard, by way of masculine decoration. On this fateful evening, the newly engaged couple walked in the door to the apartment to find both of the items had been forcefully ripped from the wall and were now in the middle of the floor standing upright in a tepee-type fashion.

Matt noted, "You couldn't move the lacrosse stick on the wall because it was bolted in place. You'd have had to get a screwdriver to remove it, and the same with the skateboard. And this stuff was in the middle of the floor, like it had been strategically placed. We had locks and deadbolts. You aren't getting into this place without somebody knowing it."

"We hadn't been gone all that long," he continued, "and the house felt different." While he admitted that it never felt particularly good in the house, even on a good day, it felt particularly bad that afternoon. Matt walked through the house and called out to the spirits: "All right, if you're here, give me a sign."

According to Matt, something or someone seemed to be willing to do just that. Noelle had an alarm clock in the master bedroom that malfunctioned in a rather spectacular fashion that evening. It included a feature that would wake the sleeper with a verbal phrase, such as "wake up, sleepyhead," instead of the annoying electronic alarm that most do. If a user simply wanted to know the time, she or he could depress a button and the instrument would announce the time. But, apparently, if one wanted to change settings on the instrument, the user had to continue to depress the same menu button for several seconds before a voice prompt would come on with the message, "How can I help you?" Then, if you waited, the instrument would go through the menu options with additional button pushes. Matt admitted that it took time for the program to go through its various menu options.

This particular afternoon, the alarm clock didn't follow its prescribed protocol, but instead, without the menu button being pushed, asked, "How can I help you?" Matt wandered the apartment in somewhat of a panic. "If you're our ghost, then give us a sign." The alarm clock would respond with the unhelpful "How can I help you?"

He described, "Noelle can contest to this, as she saw it firsthand. We might actually have tape of it—I might have brought my phone out—but the alarm clock answered me, 'How can I help you?' And I hadn't actually hit the button. It doesn't even talk to you unless you hit a button, so that was the worst part. So this thing was talking to me without me even touching it. It did it once, and then it did it again. So I'm asking this thing, and it's going off." Matt estimated that this happened five or six times, and only when Matt requested a sign.

"We're both completely freaked out, so I unplugged the thing and wound up the cord and shoved the thing in the closet. I figure if this thing goes off again, I'm going to blast it with a 12-gauge." The alarm clock remains coiled up and thrust in the closet to this day. It came out only one other night, the night of the investigation, when the team Matt had brought in decided to put the alarm clock to the test.

Thoroughly frightened, Matt did what many Americans do when stressed: he grabbed his laptop, sat down on the couch, and googled exorcisms and house blessings. An avowed agnostic, Matt said he found himself walking from room to room reading the Lord's Prayer. Meanwhile, Noelle went into the master bedroom and quickly came out screaming. She told Matt that she'd seen a woman, an older woman, in their room. "Noelle is a lot of things, but she's not a bullshitter," said Matt. "If she said she saw a woman in our room, she saw a woman in our room. She was scared—she was legitimately scared. You can't fake scared. We didn't sleep in the bedroom for a week after."

Renne was renting out the mother-in-law suite in back at the time. She'd had experiences as well, including the day when she'd been bent over feeding her dog in the kitchen, and the top to a covered candle came sailing down inexplicably from a shelf, landing at her feet. Noelle and Matt discussed the happenings of their engagement evening with Renne and the three of them decided it was time to take some action. Soon after, Matt contacted a paranormal group that came out to the house and conducted an investigation.

As a favor, Matt invited Renne and me over to see the property: a small, rather unremarkable structure overshadowed by the barn, which would be more aptly labeled a large metal pole building than the traditional animal barn of old. Once again I was struck with how our perception of a haunted structure is so far off the mark of reality. We walked briefly through the small front apartment, during which time I didn't really sense anything, and then we gathered around Matt's kitchen table, where he offered to let us see the evidence the paranormal group gathered.

It had been the winter of 2011, and a local paranormal group consisting of four women came out and investigated the property. Matt informed me that he had personally killed the power in the house at the breaker box before he left. The whole family vacated the building, although Matt and a friend sat throughout the investigation in his car in the driveway.

Renne explained that the team had three solid EVPs and a video recording of the alarm clock malfunctioning. "It went off and there was no power in the house," Matt added. Renne then showed me the short video clip. Caught on the IR camera, the clip clearly shows the infamous alarm clock coming on by itself, just as Matt had reported.

Then Renne told me about the three EVPs the team had caught. All three appeared to be the same speakers, a boy and a man, Renne said. "In the one caught in the in-law suite, it sounded like the two were having an entire conversation. You hear the man's voice say 'okay,' and then the boy's voice said something that sounded like a clipped 'What are they doin'?'" I recalled that Matt had noted that all the investigators that evening were women.

In the second clip that Renne and Matt played for me, there appeared to be the same adult male voice whispering; again the words were relatively indistinguishable but may have been "lock keyed." I can only guess that perhaps the male entity wondered why strangers were wandering the premises. "He probably wondered how in the heck they'd gotten a key," Matt speculated.

According to Renne, the third EVP was the prize of the evening. Clustered around Matt's kitchen table, the three of us passed around the headphones as we each listened to the EVP. With what I heard, I had to agree with Renne. The EVP was remarkable for its length and content. Again, it captured the same two voices, the adult male voice and the voice of a boy. The voices appeared to be discussing the team of investigators and the need to stay hidden from them. The first voice, the adult male, seemed to say, "Great." (As if in a sarcastic way, like "*Great*, they're invading our space.") The child's voice then said, "We better be quiet." And then the male voice responded, "Yes, we better be."

"That clip is crystal clear. There's no mistaking what they're saying," Renne pointed out. I had to agree with her summation; the clip left little doubt what the pair had been talking about.

Renne continued to explain that she had listened to the clips several times, and she'd noted that the tone quality was consistent throughout all three. "It's clearly the same two speakers in all three clips. Remarkable consistency." I had to agree with Renne. The several sentence exchanges were incredible. Usually EVPs consist of one or two words, but this EVP was clearly an exchange between two people and continued for several sentences. And even more remarkable was the fact that none of the investigators was male, and no one else was in the building at the time—or so Matt had informed me.

I also found the amount of intelligence displayed fascinating. These two entities appeared to know that there were strangers in the house and devised a plan to avoid contact with them: "We better be quiet" and "Yes, we better be" said volumes about their intentions. Parapsychologists tend to feel that hauntings are mainly unintelligent. They reason that spirits can't change or adapt to their environment. They believe that spirits have no real concept of time or short-term memory. And this seems true for much of the evidence I gather.

So much appears to be short words like *yes* or *no* or words parroted back in response to what we'd just said. But occasionally, I'll come across evidence such as this, evidence that demonstrates an awareness of environment and a desire to adapt to the situation.

Matt said that one of the women on the team had identified herself as a medium. She told Matt and Noelle that she felt the dwelling had three spirits in attendance. One was an older woman spirit, who the psychic felt was protective and benign. There was also a teenage boy present, who the psychic said hadn't been associated with the house but with the land thereabouts. She speculated that perhaps there was an unmarked grave somewhere in the area.

And then there was an angry male spirit, who the psychic said was the one that caused the most trouble.

I don't know how much of the evidence and history of the property the medium had been privy to beforehand. However, the apparition of the older woman had been witnessed by both Noelle and Alexa, and the three EVPs we listened to all appeared to be an older male and a male child, making the psychic's conclusions interesting to say the least.

Before departing, the group performed a cleansing ritual and put salt down, according to Matt. "The place was quieter after that. They're still here, but there's not crazy stuff happening anymore."

Postscript

It has been some years now since Matt and Noelle's fateful engagement day fright. Matt surmised that the worst of the activity had happened during that four-to-five-month period around the time that Noelle and Alexa had moved in and when he and Noelle had gotten engaged. He noted that the house was quieter now, though he still felt there were presences in the home. He told me that he still occasionally caught a figure out of the corner of his eye in the hallway. "I have really good peripheral vision, and there'll be times when I'll be sitting in the other room and I'll catch movement in the hall. Alexa and Noelle will be fast asleep, the dog will be asleep, and I'll see it. I know I saw something. I just can't prove it." And the family still hears occasional footsteps in the attic. He also said the dark feeling he's often felt in the house continued. He likened it to a dimming of light in the entire building. "It's like wearing sunglasses. You step in here and it's just dimmer, darker than it should be. All the walls are painted in light colors and the ceilings are white, and yet it's always dim in here. You get the feeling of dread." He concluded, "It felt like something bad happened in there at some time. That's the best way I can describe it."

The only other truly terrifying event happened late one snowy night. Noelle and Alexa had gone to bed and were fast asleep. Matt had stayed up and was doing something at the computer. The blind on the window overlooking the porch was open so Matt could watch the idyllic snowclad landscape. He looked up from his computer to look out the window at one point, and there staring in at him was a large man whom Matt estimated at six foot to six foot two. It was dim on the porch, according to Matt. There were only a couple of lights on the porch and they weren't terribly bright. So the front of the figure was shadowed, and Matt couldn't clearly make out any features. When pressed, Matt said he felt it had been a big white man with a halo of hair, no hat. "And he was just dead still, staring in at me." The figure was solid and threatening—so solid that Matt was convinced it was a trespasser. At the time, Matt said, there'd been a less than savory apartment building just up the street from the house.

The family had had problems in the past with interlopers crossing the property. In fact, Matt had come home one day and caught a man in the act of trying to break into the house. Matt had wrestled the man down and called the cops, only to find that the man had stabbed another man up the street and was attempting to allude authorities.

So when Matt looked up and saw a man staring at him from his front porch window, his first thought was that the explanation was natural, not supernatural. He sat for a shocked moment staring at the man staring at him through the porch window. "I looked and I just couldn't believe what I was seeing, so I just sat and stared at him for what felt like a long while but was probably only a few seconds. And he wasn't moving, he wasn't going anywhere. And I wondered just how long he'd been staring in at me, whether he had been casing the joint." Then Matt bolted to the table where his rifle was sitting. A collector of firearms, he'd been working on the weapon only an hour before, and in one fluid motion headed to the front door. He didn't want to be accosted coming out the door, so Matt said he ducked in and out a couple of times just in case, and then he bolted out the front door onto the porch. Of course, the man was already gone. Matt was determined to catch him before he got too far. So he ran down the porch steps and started running around the house. If the guy tried to get in the window at the girls, he was going to seriously regret it. However, as Matt was running, his mind started to register a fact. There were no footprints in the snow, except for his own. It was a deep snow, and Matt estimated it at a foot. Any footprints would have been obvious. So the man hadn't come this way. Matt finished the circuit around the house just to be certain and then returned to the front porch. There below the window, remarkably, was fresh, pristine, unmarked snow. There were no footprints on the driveway. There were no footprints on the front lawn. No footprints, except his own, did he find anywhere on the property that evening.

"That was some time ago now," said Matt. But yet, just recently, the new tenant in the mother-in-law suite approached Matt with a query. A musician from Key West, he knew little about the Berlin area. He came up to Matt one day and asked outright, "This place is haunted, isn't it?"

Matt doesn't tell prospective tenants that the place is haunted. "It wouldn't be good for business. And yet all the tenants ask me at some time whether the place is haunted. So it happens to this day."

CHAPTER 7
THE DETERMINED NURSE

Lewes, Delaware

A residual haunt, while it can be quite shocking, will not exhibit the same characteristics of an intelligent haunting. If you witness the apparition, it will not interact with you or appear to notice you at all. It's merely a recording of a past event. Such appeared to be the case in the story below.

Our group was invited to set up a vendor table at a haunted pop-up in Lewes, Delaware, one Halloween season. The short, one-day event featured vendors selling Ouija boards and books about ghosts and the like. Actually, I wasn't selling much of anything but was sitting fairly idly at my table when a man approached me. I asked him if he'd like to fill out our survey, which he respectfully declined to do.

"So you investigate hauntings?" he asked.

"Yes, that's what we do. We're paranormal investigators."

"Well, I have a story for you. It's my story."

The author outside the haunted pop-up in Lewes, Delaware.

As he leaned in conspiratorially toward my table I found that was all the precursor I was to get before he launched into a truly amazing story.

He'd been a laboratory technician working a night shift in an old hospital. He was busy one night spinning his centrifuges and filling test tubes and doing whatever else lab technicians do when alone in the dead of the night. Suddenly, he spotted a nurse, a very determined nurse, walking down the hall. The old hospital had large semicircle arched windows separating the lab area from the hall, so he could clearly see the nurse walking past one archway after another, walking quickly as if on an errand. Her skirts flowing past her and the click of her heels on the floor were evidence that she had a job to do, and she was going to get it done.

One of his duties as a lab tech was to check out blood, as needed, to the nurses. He recalled that she was wearing a gray dress and a sort of white cap on her head as she headed toward the blood bank.

Not wanting to get in trouble, he left his post at the laboratory and headed quickly to the blood bank, only to find no nurse waiting impatiently for him when he arrived. He was worried. So he went upstairs and asked the first nurse he found what had happened to the nurse he'd seen walking toward the blood bank. She looked confused; apparently, there'd been no recent need for blood. She asked him what the nurse he'd seen had been wearing. He told her she'd been in a gray dress with a white cap.

The nurse looked at him oddly.

"What's wrong?" he asked. "Really, if there was a nurse that needed blood, I need to find her and make sure she gets what she needs."

"Are you sure you saw a nurse in that kind of uniform?"

"I know what I saw. Can you please tell me which nurse on which floor is looking for blood?"

"You do understand that nurses haven't worn that type of uniform in at least forty years," she said.

He was perplexed to say the least. Apparently, the nurse he had witnessed had been so solid and lifelike, not to mention determined, that he'd never even questioned in his mind that what he had seen was real, despite the fact that her garb was exceptionally odd by modern medical standards.

Final Assessment

"That was my experience," he said and left without giving me his name or any other information. Sometimes gifts such as this simply fall into your lap. What do I take from his experience? The nurse was probably a residual haunt. The fact that the specter was so real in appearance that he never questioned her existence is remarkable. But I feel our lab tech was probably in the right spot at the exact right time to witness this nurse from the past.

A quick perusal of the history of nursing uniforms seemed to indicate that the nurse was probably dressed as an American nurse around the time of World War I. At the time, nurses wore a gray cotton crepe material uniform with a double collar or wing collar and white cuffed sleeves.

Although my witness didn't mention it, they also often wore a Red Cross insignia on their cap, pin, or brassard to make them easily identifiable on the battlefield or in battle hospitals.

At the turn of the twentieth century, nurses wore head coverings reminiscent of nuns' with a full cap and veil. As this can't have been practical to wartime nursing, the fashions eventually gave way to the classic winged white cap that many of us still associate with nurses.

Consider also the hem length of the skirt. Dress lengths were becoming shorter by necessity, as a nurse needed maneuverability in a war zone. So dress lengths shortened first to the lower calf and eventually to midcalf. I wonder if this isn't close to the nursing uniform the witness described. Nursing uniforms didn't become predominantly white until World War II, if you're wondering. World War I, the Great Depression, the Roaring Twenties—all these eras with their residual energy might have been prime contributors for embedding energy into the edifices of an old hospital, and our unwitting lab tech became witness to a snapshot out of time.

CHAPTER 8
WHEN THOMAS CAME TO VISIT

I believe that it is a common misconception that a spirit is stuck in one location. While this is true of a residual haunting, in which an event is recorded and becomes imbedded into the environment, it is not necessarily true of an intelligent spirit, who can move about freely at the speed of thought.

I find even my investigators dig too often into the history of the property, thinking they'll find clues to the identity of a spirit, convinced that a property needs have a dark past in order to be haunted. Who died on the property? What tragedy befell a home that precipitated the haunting?

In my research, I've often found evidence that spirits seem to move about as freely as their human counterpoints. If the home in which they resided for years gets torn down, they'll seemingly move to another structure—for example, often one that is close to the original building. Such appeared to be the case in our Long Neck investigation, in which a spirit in a long skirt and a ruffled collar blouse in 1800s style, her hair in a bun, seemed to be haunting a 1970s ranch built on otherwise undeveloped land.

Spirits may also travel to visit loved ones or even strangers who pique their interest. Investigators report unwittingly attracting the attention of a spirit who then follows them home. Hence, a home that has never had paranormal activity suddenly does, much to the chagrin of the living inhabitants. Certainly, if you're in the business that I am in, you often open yourself up for such experiences whether wittingly or unwittingly.

This was the case for my own family for a few months, when we seemed to have acquired a surprise house guest. Our house in Felton, Delaware, is relatively new construction. Built on a property that had once been a farm, the house now stands near to where the cow barn used to be. Indeed, on very rainy days we still often smell the scent of cow manure. Digging in the area, we have found the remnants of old tools and broken pieces of china. Once, while putting in a patio, we found the remains of what we surmised to be the family dog, shrouded in an old quilt. Apparently, the property had its own tragic past, as the farmer who had owned the farm committed suicide by jumping off the barn when he received the news that he was terminally ill with cancer. The death shocked the community. Still, our house was without paranormal activity—until a friend of the family passed away.

When Thomas Came to Visit

I worked for a year in the therapy and rehabilitation department of a nursing home. It was a truly unique experience working with the geriatric population.

Many of them loved to talk, and their lives were often fascinating. I met a woman who had hand-sewn the space gloves for the likes of Buzz Aldrin and Neil Armstrong, and a congenial man who still bore shrapnel in his leg from fighting in World War II. And then there was Thomas...

Thomas was charismatic and gregarious. He was a wonderful storyteller and had a sense of humor that often had me roaring with laughter. Then again, he also had a stubborn streak that defied understanding, and even at the age of eighty-one, he expected to be the man in charge. Most of all, he had that gift, which so few people possess, of making you feel like there was no one in the world with whom he would rather be. He was also solidly and unapologetically a devoted old lecher who flirted with every female of the species he ever came across. He was good with women; he liked and understood them.

Thomas's other great passion was cars. His entire life had revolved around these wonderful machines, and many of his stories were about the vehicles he loved. He had been a highly respected mechanic, and for decades he'd built and serviced his own race cars. He and his son had both driven them, but when he realized he didn't have the aptitude as a race car driver, he'd hired one and financed the racing team.

He'd had two very eventful marriages. His second wife had been twenty years his junior and only a few months older than his eldest son, a fact that caused some consternation in the family.

I worked with Thomas for a number of weeks, during which time we became very close. When the day came that he was discharged from therapy, I found that I missed our conversations. When lunchtime came, I found myself taking my peanut butter sandwich down the hall to Thomas's room. We shared a love of peanut butter. Our friendship survived until his death. I'd moved on to a different job by that time, but I still visited him when I could, dropping by on a Friday afternoon. Then one sad Friday, I went to his room to find someone else in his bed and his belongings gone. I asked at the desk, though I feared the answer. He'd passed away earlier in the week.

I had been a paranormal investigator when I knew him, and I often invited him to visit me after he passed, to let me know he was still around. When strange things started occurring around the house, therefore, it wasn't a complete surprise.

It was late one night, with my husband asleep beside me, when I heard a distinctly loud, breathy voice from the bathroom exclaim, "Yes!" I remember it was so distinct that I lifted my head off the pillow and asked if there was anyone there. I got no reply.

One Saturday morning shortly after, I heard a large bang coming again from the master bathroom. I thought something had fallen, but I never found the source of the bang.

My father had adopted a hobby of repairing old clocks, the wind-up kind, after he retired. His collection of old clocks grew so large that he gave a few of them to me. Two of his mantel clocks I carefully keep wound and running all the time. One afternoon I decided to wind the clocks, only to find both of them were set an hour ahead. If you've dealt with old clocks you know that they have a way of running slow, sometimes profoundly slow. To find them running an hour ahead, therefore, was really bizarre. The evidence that something odd was going on was starting to mount.

Then one evening my husband and I were lying in bed together. I was reading a book and he was on his laptop. We were both very much awake. My husband suddenly asked me, "Did you just move your feet?"

"No," I replied, wondering why he asked. "I've just been lying here quietly." I went back to reading.

A couple of minutes later he again asked, "Did you just move your feet?"

"No," I again replied. "Why do you ask?"

"Because it felt like someone just sat down on the edge of the bed right by my feet."

"That's weird," I said. "But no, I haven't moved." I went back to reading.

Suddenly my husband jumped out of bed and walked very quickly into the master bathroom. The leap out of bed was so abrupt and out of character I immediately asked, "What are you doing? What's wrong?"

With a look of utter confusion on his face he replied, "It just felt like something pinched my leg." My husband is not the kind to be easily rattled, and he doesn't count every odd occurrence as being something supernatural, so when he reported being pinched by an unknown quantity, I tended to believe him.

Odd things had started to occur so regularly that I began keeping a log of the events, as I suggest my clients do. Then one Saturday, I held a meeting for the paranormal group at my house. We had a couple of new members and a lot of new equipment to learn, and I wanted us to do a trial run before our first official investigation. A couple of the members were experimenting with their new Mel Meters, measuring electromagnetic fields and ambient temperature. Another member and I were attempting to get the new surveillance camera system up and running. It's one of the great joys of my life, trying to figure out new electronic equipment (*deep sarcasm*). So I was otherwise engaged with the system's interface, a florid torrent of questionable language flowing freely. Thus, I wasn't paying attention to the women as they wandered around my house with their Mel Meters.

At one point they asked if they could go out in my overstuffed garage. They'd gotten a strange EMF spike in my kitchen that appeared to have disappeared out the wall. Reluctantly I told them they could, wondering what could possibly be of interest out there. They came back in a few minutes later, very excited. They'd gotten a seven-point spike in the garage. I really didn't think much of it, concentrating still on the incomprehensible computer interface of the DVR.

We finally got the cameras up and operating, and we all sat down with our meters and voice recorders and did a short dress rehearsal of an EVP session. We were packing up when one of the team members, Maya, came up to me with a question. She asked me what I thought of mastiffs.

"Mastiffs? They're really big dogs. That's about all I know. Why?" I asked, rather stymied.

"That's the picture I get in my head. He looks kind of like a mastiff."

"Who?" I asked, now thoroughly bewildered.

"The man I see. Remember I said we'd gotten those EMF spikes. I think it's the man who looks kind of like a mastiff." And then it dawned on me. Thomas had been of Germanic descent and build, with a thick head of blond hair. At six feet plus, he might have given the impression of a large beast. I went to my office desk and fished out a picture I had of him. I showed Maya the photo. She looked at it for a while and then said, "Yes, I think that's him, but he's younger now. He's more like fifty years old. Oh, and he's happy we're talking about him now. He's happy you know he's here."

A few nights later, in a very private session, I told Thomas that he didn't have to stick around on my account. It was then that I thought I felt a brush on my hand. In ten plus years of investigating, I'd never felt a touch before. But I did that night. I was awe-struck. After our "talk" the activity became less frequent and less intense, eventually ceasing altogether. Thomas had moved on.

CHAPTER 9
SCREAMS IN THE GLOAMING

Marydel, Delaware

I became acquainted with Nick when he applied for membership with my paranormal research group. Like many of my applicants, he'd had several experiences that had piqued his interest in the paranormal. One story in particular I found fascinating, as it appeared to demonstrate how sometimes it's not buildings but the land itself that is haunted.

This region of the country that I now call home has a rich history. The first settlement in Delaware was not surprisingly a coastal one. Now known as Lewes, the first town in Delaware was established in 1631 by the Dutch. Settlers soon found that the land was fertile and the climate warm enough for long growing seasons. A recent archeological find west of Rehoboth, Delaware, revealed eleven unmarked graves from the Avery's Rest plantation. One of the first plantations in Delaware, if not the first, it was established in the mid-1600s when John Avery and his family emigrated from Maryland to Delaware. They would establish an eight-hundred-acre plantation, growing mainly a cash crop of tobacco that gave Avery both wealth and a standing within the community. Other settlers would soon follow.

Of course, European settlers were not the first to inhabit the area. Before the European settlers arrived, the Lenni Lenape tribes, meaning "genuine people" in the Algonquian language, traversed Delaware, New Jersey, New York, and Pennsylvania for several thousand years. The colonists renamed them the Delaware Indians for the Delaware River that ran across the region. The Lenni Lenape took advantage of the rich soil, growing corn, squash, beans, sweet potatoes, and tobacco. They established their communities near waterways and erected permanent homes, rectangular bark covered buildings called longhouses. As the colonists descended on them in ever increasing numbers, the Indians were sadly forced westward, sometimes peacefully, sometimes not.

The courageous war leader Pontiac attempted to unite the tribes during the 1760s into an army whose purpose was to drive the colonists from their lands. He was defeated in 1763 by the English. Today, many of the descendants of the Delaware Indians live in Oklahoma, far from their native coastal lands, the waterways, the sea breezes, and the abundant soil. Lumped into the Cherokee nation, who were also herded to the Oklahoma region, the Delaware Indians were not recognized as their own tribe until the 1960s.

Some of the native people, such as the Nanticoke tribe now headquartered in Bridgeton, Cumberland County, New Jersey, avoided extradition and remain in the area to this day, under their own governance.

Nick recalled his childhood in an old farmhouse, which was built on land that had obviously once been inhabited by the Delaware Indians. Nick, his mother, his father, and his brother had moved to the old farmhouse when Nick was thirteen. The house, Nick explained, was in Marydel, Delaware, "within walking distance of Maryland and Mudd Mill Pond." He related that the farm belonged to his grandparents, and despite selling the farm to the Amish for use as a school, his grandfather still resided in the old farmhouse to this day.

In Nick's recounting of events, it appeared that it wasn't the farm or the house that was haunted so much as the land. When the fog rolled in and night was falling over the fields and woods that surrounded it, the land became something other than an idyllic farmstead.

Nick admitted that he believed the spirits of the Lenni Lenape still roamed the area. Over the years, the family found ample evidence to suggest that the land was once inhabited by them. "I believe it's Native American because it was Native American ground. I can't even count the number of arrowheads I've found out there." Nick recalled that every spring when the fields were plowed for planting and the ground churned, new arrowheads were found.

The farmstead's location is also historically significant for the fact that the Mason-Dixon Line ran right through the land. Surveyed from 1763 to 1767, the Mason-Dixon Line became the boundary between Pennsylvania, Maryland, and Delaware, the infamous demarcation line between the free states of the North and the slave states of the South.

Nick recalled that he and his brother loved to explore the woods, as boys so often do. Nick in particular enjoyed long walks in the woods. But he admitted that even in daylight he often encountered strange shadowy figures. "I'd sometimes see things moving around, but there wasn't actually anything there." He also remembered hearing noises of passage through the leafy confines for which he could not account.

The woods were actually part of the property, so anyone in the woods would have been trespassing, not that people don't trespass often. But Nick continued, "Grandpa had owned forty-five acres at the time, and it had been a field and then the farmland and then the woods, so someone on foot would have had to travel quite a distance to get to the woods." And he noted that the nearest neighbors didn't have children. Homeless people will often take up residence in an isolated area, but when asked, Nick noted that he had never seen a homeless person nor evidence of such in the woods either.

"We would always see the shadows. We would hear the movement. In the woods, it would often happen during the day. But at night, when the fog rolled in, we would see full-on shadows moving between the light and throughout the fog itself. They were human height. A couple of them were like six three. On special nights when it was really cool outside in the summer, the fog would roll in over the top of the field. And there would be just enough moonlight to shine down into the fog. It would be a really thick fog because it's an open area and the woods are right there, and that tends to happen with the moisture."

Nick continued, "I spent most of my time outside, up on the mound where our septic system is or up in our tree house." From there, Nick said, it was possible to look directly down at the field. He said he would see multiple figures in the fog. "And they'd be spread out like they were running. Or sometimes we'd see them, and they'd just be casually walking through the fog. But it would be spread out. You'd see a bunch here, and sometimes over here you'd see a bunch there, and they would just seem to dart back and forth past each other. It would go on for a good while, and it was always around the same time when it was most active. It was about eleven thirty when it started, and it would end around one thirty to two o'clock. Around three o'clock in the morning, everything would calm down, and you'd have this really unusual, uneasy feeling about the whole thing, because it would just be this unnervingly calm, quiet," he described.

Summer, Nick concluded, was the time when most of the activity seemed to occur. The family's Jack Russell Terrier seemed to detect something as well. The dog would often stop in the yard, staring off in the same direction as the boys, toward the fields and the woods. Sometimes he would growl or bark at the shadowy figures moving about in the fog.

In the House

While Nick said that the majority of the activity happened in the woods or in the fields, at least occasionally strange things would happen in the house as well. "My dad thought it was us, but sometimes we'd have stuff fall off the walls in the house. We had one really large picture, probably about that size," he noted, pointing at my large mantel picture, which measured about two and three-quarters by three and a half feet. "It was definitely secured on the wall. And it just dropped. My brother and I weren't doing anything at all. He was asleep, and I was on my bed reading a book." For no apparent reason, the large picture just came crashing down.

On one memorable occasion, Nick noted, he had experienced undeniable proof of something paranormal within the house. "I came home from school and I was worried that my mom was going to kick my butt because my grades weren't exactly satisfactory on my report card." His mother, who was working a night shift, wasn't home, so Nick was waiting up for her to come home.

"I would say it was probably ten thirty or eleven o'clock, about a half hour before she got home." Nick was lying in his small, twin-size bed when he "felt this really hard pressure, which seriously felt like somebody's foot was pushing me in the rear end, and I fell over to the other side of the bed." Upon examination, there were no marks found on his body. Still, he said, "There was no mistaking it: I was hit."

Not asleep when it happened, Nick recalled he was simply lying in bed contemplating what he would say about his grades when his mother got home. Nick remembered thinking, *Oh boy, what is going to happen here?* "And then out of nowhere … I got kicked. Nothing moved, nothing got changed—I just got kicked directly out of bed. It was one of those things. You could not deny it … It was a full-blown hit."

Screams in the Gloaming

The apex of the frightening events occurred one evening in late July. The events of that evening would shock the family to the core. As Nick recalled, it happened five or six times to the family that night, at dusk. Just as the sun was in its final descent before plunging the farm into darkness, the woods already deeply shadowed, a blood-curdling scream was heard resonating across the land. It being summer, windows in the old farmhouse were open to the breezes. Nick's family was sitting in the family room at the time. When the first scream occurred, he said everyone jolted to their feet, asking what had they all just heard. And then a few minutes later, the scream was heard again. There would be several screams that evening, invading the small family's peace with their shocking violence.

The day had been a hot one, Nick recalled, in the 90s, with high humidity. But the evening had cooled down to comfortable lower 70s. "The air was still. There was no wind. You could hear the crickets, the birds settling down. We had chickens at the time.

We could hear them moving around. But then everything went dead silent. And then these screams occurred. To this day we haven't been able to figure out what that was. We all heard it. Nobody could deny it."

The preternatural stillness continued until an hour after dark, the natural night sounds muted, the shocking screams occurring again, and again, and then from the woods the family distinctly heard the sounds of branches snapping and leaves crunching. Though the house is situated, in Nick's estimation, a half mile from the woods, still the family heard the sounds from the woods as if a large animal or a ghostly army were crashing through. "We also heard noises, like something was moving around back there, but we couldn't actually see anything. So we couldn't actually see movement, but we heard a lot."

The boys attempted to investigate. Taking flashlights, they tried to follow the sounds back to the woods. Their search proved futile. They could find no sign of tracks or broken branches. They did find the remains of what Nick described as an old kill—shredded, desiccated pieces of flesh and dried blood that appeared to be from an animal killed several days before. Obviously not related to the events, it was still a grisly find for two young men already fearful in the dark woods after nightfall.

The family dog was likewise spooked. According to Nick, "When we heard those screams, he sat there for two hours growling and barking at the direction of the woods at absolutely nothing. Growling at the direction from where he'd heard the noises."

Nick concluded about that ghastly night, "None of us ever saw what it was. We just heard the screams, over and over again. It was definitely terrifying, to say the least."

Final Assessment

Whether residual or intelligent, the spirits of the former caretakers of the land likely still remained. The land on which the family farm stood had certainly been used as a hunting ground by the Native Americans, as evidenced by the numerous arrowheads the family found. The property's close proximity to water might also have meant that the Native Americans lived on or near the land as well, as my research indicated that they built their longhouses on or near the shores of waterways. And certainly, if the Native Americans lived in the area, they also died in the area. Perhaps an Indian burial ground lies there or nearby.

The figures that the boys saw running through the fog might have been residual, recordings in the environment of warriors long-since perished. The kick off the bed that Nick experienced, however, suggests an intelligent spirit, as it interacted with Nick in a very real, combative manner. Perhaps still upset from being turned off his native land, the spirit decided to take out his anger on an unwitting recipient.

The screams in the night were the most puzzling part of the story. In my interview with Nick, he admitted that his brother had done some research into the matter after that terrifying evening and decided that what the family had heard was a Native American demon or monster. But Nick couldn't recall the name that his brother had claimed it to be.

I tentatively suggested a *wendigo*. I say tentatively because suggesting a wendigo is somewhat like suggesting a vampire or bigfoot; therefore, I wanted to move carefully in my summation.

"Yes, that's the name," he agreed immediately, obviously excited that I had heard of them.

In my research after the interview, I found that the wendigo is a construct of the Algonquin tribes, of which the Lenni Lenape were members. The word derived from the Algonquin root word *witiku*, meaning "evil spirit" or "cannibal." The Ojibwe variant of the word is *windigo*. Such creatures share similar characteristics with the werewolf and vampire, being creatures who feed on humans and change their forms. It was believed that a hunter lost or abandoned in the woods without food could become a wendigo. In such form, he would seek out the flesh of humans on which to feed. A wendigo might appear in the form of a crazed Native American warrior breathing flames, or it might take the guise of a supernatural monster with a heart of ice that flies through nighttime forests in search of a victim. The Ojibwe think of it as a terrifying ogre that steals away children who do not behave. It appears capable, in any case, of shapeshifting. Appearing in the mythology of northern Native Americans from the Atlantic Ocean westward to the Rocky Mountains and into Canada as far north as Quebec, stories of these monsters abound. And not all the accounts are old.

There are numerous variations on the stories of these creatures who were said to hunt most often solitarily and silently. But then on some nights, lonely hunters and trappers huddled in their remote cabins would recount that they heard bloodcurdling screams in the dark. In the morning, they would find large trees torn down and boulders moved around with apparent ease. It seemed that on these occasions the wendigo went out of its way to make the humans aware of its passing.

I was rather stunned to find the similarities with the legend of the wendigo and the account of the event as described by Nick. The family had heard both the frightening screams and the sounds of violent activity in the woods. He also described the preternatural silence of the night, the muted night sounds of bugs and animals that are often associated with supernatural events. Had the family heard the evidence of the passage of a supernatural creature across their land? Indeed, what monsters might roam in the dark of night?

CONCLUSION

When people find out what I do in my off hours, they're often fascinated or appalled. I inevitably get asked the same questions: Did you ever see or experience anything? What is the most frightening thing that ever happened to you? Obviously, I wouldn't still be investigating the paranormal if I'd never experienced anything. I would have quickly become bored and probably been forced to take up golf. But when I'm at my computer and I find that little nugget of gold in the audio, see an object shoot off the shelf in an empty room on the video, or watch an unseen force seemingly move about the room setting off our detectors, I still get the same chill up my spine as I did on my first investigation. These small gems make up for the late nights I sit in a dark house when nothing occurs and the hours of audio and video I peruse in which absolutely nothing happens.

I can now say that odd things happen to otherwise normal people, people from all walks of life. Very often there appears no rhyme or reason to the happenings.

While the answers aren't always obvious, I have noticed that periods of change or upheaval are very often involved. Renovations to a home or a structure are very often associated with an uptick in paranormal activity, hence the surprised exclamation I get from homeowners when I ask the question, as I do with every interview. Yes, they admit, it all started when they remodeled the bathroom or tore out the old kitchen.

For others it begins as soon as they move into a building, as if the spirit or spirits had grown used to the status quo and suddenly there is a new dynamic involved. The bottom line: spirits don't seem to be fond of change.

Most often the activity that people experience is more startling than terrifying. The ubiquitous footfalls and electrical disturbances are so common as to be almost cliché. An apparition may eventually be witnessed, though it's rare to see a full-bodied apparition straight on. Normally, witnesses admit to sensing movement or catching a shadowy shape out of the corner of their eye. This leaves the witness confused about whether they actually saw something or simply imagined it. I think this type of cat-and-mouse game is perhaps intentional on the part of the spirit. They want you to know that they're there. In some ways, they want the attention, while in other ways, they simply want to be left alone.

I say this from experience. On numerous investigations we've done, we've sat for hours trying to encourage a spirit to interact with us, but almost nothing occurs. We leave thinking the night was a complete disaster, only to find we have a gold mine on evidence review. We'll catch disembodied voices and objects moving in empty rooms. In one recent but remarkable case, while the team was outside the dwelling, the sound of a door being scraped against the floor and then slammed shut was caught three times in quick succession in an upstairs bedroom, in what appeared to be some type of ghostly temper tantrum. Video of the same bedroom showed no movement at all. The mysterious sounds were so loud that they were picked up on audio recorders placed downstairs in the home.

Rarer is the phenomenon of objects actually moving, disappearing, or reappearing in odd places. Then there is the occasional touchy-feely spirit who may brush the top of a head or a hand. In some cases, witnesses have even been scratched. Most of the time, what people experience is confusing, leaving the person wondering if it really happened. I'm here to tell you it isn't always your imagination.

After more than a decade of investigating, I can say that really odd things do occur to normal people every day. While skeptics and scientists may try to dismiss events with rational explanations, I know that there are still some mysteries in this world that have not been fully solved. These are mysteries not of solid matter, but raw energy, mysteries most often just below our senses. There are voices of past lives and past events that want to be heard, even if the message is simply "We are here—do not forget us." I'm here and I'm trying to listen. Because, in the end, I believe the world is full of ghosts.

GLOSSARY

Data Logger. The data logger records multiple changes in the environment and records them. It detects and records temperature, barometric pressure, humidity, EMF, vibration, and so on. It has lights that light up to alert an investigator of abrupt changes in the area. It takes minute by minute readings of a room and records all the data in spreadsheet format. The file can be opened in a graphing software, offering an immediate picture of the investigation. Other developed computer-based data-logging systems can run into the thousands of dollars. Our team utilizes the EDI data logger, which is a small, handheld, stand-alone device, and I like it not only for the price but also for the portability. I can afford several of them and then place them in myriad locations throughout an investigation.

Disembodied Voice. Disembodied voices are voices that you hear on an investigation with your own ears but that weren't produced by a living person or known source. They may or may not be picked up on an audio recorder.

Dowsing Rods. Dowsing rods are an ancient divining tool. As such, they have a long history and many uses, most notably to find sources of water or mineral deposits. They can be as simple as a single forked branch or as complicated as rods with finely worked materials. Mine are brass rods bent in an L shape with loose wooden handles that allow the rods to move and spin without hindrance.

Dowsing rods have been studied for many years by those who wish to dismiss their use as completely superstitious. Perhaps most notably, the Society for Psychical Research conducted studies on the use of dowsers and were unable to arrive at a decisive conclusion.

I use dowsing rods to give me a sense of the energy in an area. Sometimes, under lucky circumstances, I've also been able to use them to have yes/no conversations with a suspected entity. Crossed rods indicate a yes answer, and uncrossing rods indicate a no or neutral answer. Therefore, if I ask a question such as "Are you a man?" and the rods do not move, we take that as a no. If I then ask if the entity is a woman and they cross, we take that as a yes. In between questions and answers, I request the rods return to a neutral uncrossed position.

Dowsing rods are fascinating, if a little creepy. The fact that an inanimate object will move or spin on its own is incredible, although scientists suspect that the rods actually move because of muscular micromovements of your arms and hands.

Electromagnetic Energy. Electromagnetic energy is energy emitted or reflected from objects in the waves both electrical and magnetic. These waves can travel through space. There is electromagnetic energy that occurs naturally at the core of the earth's surface. Our brains and our muscles are powered by low levels of electromagnetic energy, produced by chemical changes. Certainly, our electronic devices from lamps to iPods utilize electromagnetic energy in order to function.

Broadly stated, it is energy that is both magnetic, meaning it moves from a positive pole to a negative pole, and electric, meaning a negative electron or ion moves through space. The two forces move together in waves. Basically all energy can be graphed on a spectrum. The lower end of the spectrum has looser waves with the crests further apart. At the low end of the spectrum are the extremely low frequency (ELF) electromagnetic fields of AC power, which we use to power most of our electric appliances. Above that are the intermediate frequency fields (IF) with the wave crests closer together. This is the radio wave and microwave portion of the spectrum. The infrared spectrum is just below what is visible light to humans. Just beyond the visible light spectrum are the ultraviolet rays. Undoubtedly, you've heard of ultraviolet rays in connection with using sunscreen on a hot day. These light rays are faster moving and thus have more energy, which can be harmful to exposed flesh.

Electricity can be static. For instance, when you break the electrical circuit by turning off a light switch, the electrons that would normally be shifting down the circuit from one atom to the next stall out and merely rotate around their own nucleus. Magnetism can also be static. Consider the magnets you use to pin important pictures to the refrigerator. However, when electricity and magnetism become coupled and one of these forces changes, it causes a change in the other force. Both begin moving together in waves—electromagnetic waves. The magnetic and electric fields of an electromagnetic wave are perpendicular to each other and to the direction in which the wave is moving.

Electromagnetic waves appear impervious to such concerns as gravitation or friction. Once created, an electromagnetic wave will continue moving forever unless it becomes absorbed by matter.

Electromagnetic Field Detector. Electromagnetic field detectors were created to measure different types of electromagnetic energy. Some were created to measure AC fields, which are the fields emitted from man-made devices that require electrical wiring to operate, such as a dishwasher or lamp. Still others measure DC fields, such as the earth's naturally occurring geomagnetic field or cell phones. These devices are known as Gauss meters or magnetizers.

Electronic Voice Phenomenon (EVP). An EVP is a voice that is captured on an audio recording device that you don't hear with your own ears. Experts in EVPs believe that such recordings are imprinted into the recording device versus being actual sounds caught on the machine. Why the distinction? Ghosts, they contend, don't have a body, and therefore they do not have vocal cords. Hence, they can't actually speak. Sometimes these voices will seem to be answering your questions, often they will appear to parrot back what you just said, and then sometimes they seem to have their own agenda.

I have had a long love affair with the EVP: first, because researchers have been able to conduct experiments in soundproofed, radio-frequency-blocked sound stages and still been able to capture EVPs, which argues to the fact that they are a real phenomenon; and second, because it's remarkable to play back a recording and hear a voice that clearly doesn't belong to someone on the team speaking with you.

Ghost Box. This device has been popularized by paranormal television shows. It's an instrument that scans across radio frequencies. The theory behind it is that a spirit can use the white noise and bits of conversation to form words. The problem is that there's absolutely no way a person can know with certainty that what they hear isn't a snippet of radio. Worse, I find people who use them will accept anything the things spit out as if it's the gospel truth. One enthusiastic spectator once told me, "That ghost box was amazing. It said 'car' and then right afterward a car drove by." Now, I ask you, what is the likelihood of a car driving by on a road? We're not talking Nostradamus here. I don't use ghost boxes during serious investigations. But I do allow the team to use them as a type of entertainment, like how I use my dowsing rods. As such, I don't present them as evidence to a client.

Orbs. Orbs are believed to be small balls of energy and not spirits. As a result, it's believed that they are often at or near haunted locations. For an orb to be an orb, it should emit its own light and not be reflecting other light sources, such as the flash on a still camera. It should act in a way that demonstrates some type of intelligence. It should also be spherical and not flat.

I receive more inquiries about orbs than any other type of phenomenon. So let me say for the record that I don't take stock in orbs unless—here's the caveat—they can be seen with the naked eye. Pollen, dust, humidity, bugs, cobwebs, spiderwebs—all of these are reflective, especially when caught on a camera with a flash attachment close to the lens. They're also highly reflective on cameras, such as surveillance cameras, in an infrared setting. Car headlights and flashlights and even the lights from a low-flying plane have also been mistaken for orbs.

If the circle of light appears flat in nature, it is an indication that the light source is man-made.

But an orb of light that is visible to the naked eye, appears to have some substance, and can be witnessed moving in a semi-intelligent manner is another, well, matter. Aside from ball lightning, which is still highly debated, there's no science as far as I know that can explain a ball of energy that emits its own visible light and dances around a room in some semi-intelligent fashion.

Last summer, I was sent a couple of pictures from a woman who wanted her orbs diagnosed. In the photos, there were clearly two bright green balls of light. They were giving off light and not reflecting it. I was stymied for a couple of days, and then I had an epiphany. Late summer in Delaware is lightning bug season.

To be honest, I throw out 99.9 percent of orb pictures I am sent or the team reports. To date I have never received a convincing photograph of an orb.

REM Pod. REM Pods generate a magnetic field around themselves and sound an alarm when the field is disturbed. They also detect changes in temperature. Small, stationary devices, they can be placed strategically in places reported to have high activity and alert investigators of immediate changes in the environment. Use of such devices has to be carefully monitored, however, as electronic devices such as cell phones, walkie-talkies, and remote controls can also set off the alarms.

Renovations. Renovations to a structure are often believed to be a cause of increased paranormal activity. Whether this is due to the uncovering of structures where imbedded recordings have been buried for years or the fact that a spirit doesn't like structural changes from the norm is uncertain. What is certain is that when someone starts tearing down walls or ripping out flooring, paranormal activity that might have been benign or even nonexistent up to that point can suddenly take on a much darker tone. Think about it sensibly: if someone came in to your home and started making radical changes, how would you feel? Probably uncontrollably angry. Hence, many of our investigations end up centering on the start of renovations in a building.

Water. It is a common theory among paranormal investigators that where there is water, often there is paranormal activity. A building with an open well in the basement or a building built on an underground spring may experience more supernatural activity than a building built on dry earth. That is not to say that every house built on water has activity, nor that other elements might react with water to create an amplifying effect. Still, it does entice one to wonder what it is about water that seems to sustain not only life but also the distant echoes of past lives.

To understand water, we need to look to the science of medicine. For centuries, people have used homeopathic remedies to cure ailments. Such remedies use therapeutic agents that in their natural form are so toxic that, given to a person directly, they would do more harm than good. They must be diluted, heavily diluted, with water. In many cases, the agents are so heavily diluted that the original substance is no longer traceable in the solution. Yet those who take the remedies say they often work. French scientist Jacques Benveniste made a startling discovery while doing experiments: water seems to have a memory. The mysterious substance appears to have the ability to record a substance and demonstrate its memory even after the substance is no longer present. There is a possibility that water molecules record a likeness to substances with which they have come in contact. This impressionability, this adaptability, in the element of water may be the cause of much paranormal activity. Obviously, this theory would help explain much in the way of residual haunting.

BIBLIOGRAPHY

"About." PHB Inc. General Contractors. Accessed July 22, 2017. http://www.phb-inc.com/about-1.html.

"A Magical Theory of Reality." Toteg Tribe. 2004. http://www.shadowdance.org/toteg/reality.html.

"Brief History of Fort Delaware." Delaware State Parks. Accessed July 15, 2017. http://www.destateparks.com/park/fort-delaware/civil-war/camp-trail/ (page discontinued).

Cheeseman, Ali. "Ghost Hunters Test Historic Fort." *Delaware State News*, September 30, 2008. Pages 1 and 3.

Chesapeake Ghost Walks. "The Child Spirit at the Atlantic Hotel." November 17, 2014. http://chesapeakeghostwalks.com/child-spirit-atlantic-hotel/.

Cunningham, S. A., ed. *Confederate Veteran*. Vol. 15. Nashville, TN: S. A. Cunningham Proprietor, 1907.

Greer, John Michael. *Monsters: An Investigator's Guide to Magical Beings*. St. Paul, MN: Llewellyn Publications, 2001.

Guggenheim, Bill, and Judy Guggenheim. "What Is an ADC?" *The ADC Project*. Accessed July 22, 2017. http://www.after-death.com/Pages/About/ADC.aspx.

Hawes, Jason, and Grant Wilson. *Ghost Hunters*. Season 4, episode 13, "Fort Delaware." Aired June 18, 2008, on Sci-Fi.

———. *Ghost Hunters*. "2008 Halloween Special—Ghosthunters Live." Aired October 31, 2008, on Sci-Fi.

"History." Atlantic Hotel. Accessed July 22, 2017. https://atlantichotel.com/berlin-md-hotel-history/.

Hitch, Michael. Fort Delaware Park Superintendent. Email correspondence with the author. February–March 2018.

"Lilburn Mansion." HauntedHouses.com. Accessed July 22, 2017. http://www.hauntedhouses.com/states/md/lilburn.htm.

Lipka, Michael. "18% of Americans Say They've Seen a Ghost." Pew Research Center. October 30, 2015. http://www.pewresearch.org/fact-tank/2015/10/30/18-of-americans-say-theyve-seen-a-ghost/.

Melton, Gordon J., ed. *Encyclopedia of Occultism & Parapsychology*. Vol. 2, *M–Z and Indexes*. Farmington Hills, MI: Gale Group, 2001.

Okonowicz, Ed. *Civil War Ghosts at Fort Delaware*. Elkton, MD: Myst and Lace Publishers, 2006.

Robson, David. "Psychology: The Truth about the Paranormal." *BBC Future*. October 31, 2014. http://www.bbc.com/future/story/20141030-the-truth-about-the-paranormal.

Schutte, Richard, and George C. Steitz. *Ghost Waters.* Discovery Communications, 1999. VHS, 50 min.

Seibold, David J., and Charles Adams. *Ghost Stories of the Delaware Coast.* Reading, PA: Exeter House Books, 1990.

Taylor, Troy. "Haunted Ellicott City: The Ghosts of Lilburn." *Ghosts of the Prairie.* Accessed July 22, 2017. http://www.prairieghosts.com/lilburn.html.

To Write to the Author

If you wish to contact the author or would like more information about this book, please write to the author in care of Llewellyn Worldwide, and we will forward your request. Both the author and the publisher appreciate hearing from you and learning of your enjoyment of this book and how it has helped you. Llewellyn Worldwide cannot guarantee that every letter written to the author can be answered, but all will be forwarded. Please write to:

Robin M. Strom
℅ Llewellyn Worldwide
2143 Wooddale Drive
Woodbury, MN 55125.2989

Please enclose a self-addressed stamped envelope for reply, or $1.00 to cover costs. If outside the U.S.A., enclose an international postal reply coupon.